Praise for *The Period & Puberty Parenting Revolution*

"*The Period & Puberty Parenting Revolution* is the empowering, evidence-based book you wish you had growing up: an affirming, medically accurate guide that cuts through shame and confusion so caregivers can truly show up for the kids they love during puberty and periods."

—Blair Imani, bestselling author of *Read This to Get Smarter* and creator of *Smarter in Seconds*

"Empowering and enlightening, this deeply researched and compassionate gynecological guide is a must for every family's bookshelf. Part medical memoir and part menstrual manifesto, Chambers offers a path to honest conversations with kids about gynecological health while confronting and healing the silence and trauma so many of us carry."

—Nancy Redd, *New York Times* bestselling author of *Body Drama* and *The Real Body Manual*

"*The Period & Puberty Parenting Revolution* is not just a parenting book. It's a call to action. With medical authority, cultural responsiveness, and unwavering compassion, Dr. Chambers makes clear that shame, silence, and misinformation around puberty and reproductive health are not benign. They are harmful, and they disproportionately affect communities that have long been underserved.

This book insists that medically accurate, affirming conversations are a form of care, protection, and justice. At a time when access to trusted health information is increasingly under threat, this work is both urgent and essential. Every family and every child deserves guidance rooted in truth, dignity, and respect."

—Uché Blackstock, MD, founder and CEO of Advancing Health Equity and *New York Times* bestselling author of *Legacy*

"*The Period & Puberty Parenting Revolution* is not just a book; it is an invitation for parents, especially fathers, to lean in rather than step back during one of the most important seasons of a child's life. For far too long, conversations about puberty and menstruation have excluded men, leaving girls to navigate these moments without the full support of the people who love them most. Dr. Charis Chambers dismantles shame, fear, and misinformation with clarity, compassion, and medical expertise, while offering parents a road map rooted in honesty, trust, and emotional presence. This book reminds us that being a good father is not about having all the answers; it's about showing up, listening deeply, and creating space for our daughters to feel safe, seen, and supported in their bodies. This is required reading for any parent committed to breaking generational silence, raising confident children, and redefining what it means to protect, nurture, and lead with love."

—Dr. Brandon M. Frame, founder and Chief Visionary Officer of The Black Man Can

THE PERIOD & PUBERTY PARENTING REVOLUTION

It's Time to
OWN THE CONVERSATION,
Empower Your Child, and
Rewrite the RULES OF
PARENTING KIDS Through Puberty

CHARIS CHAMBERS, MD

Cover design by Vanessa Mendozzi
Internal design by Laura Boren/Sourcebooks
Internal images © Anastasia Usenko/Getty Images, Viktoriia Kuznetsova/Getty Images, Thomas Lydell/Getty Images, Rujirat Boonyong/Getty Images, Natty Blissful/Getty Images, Michal Komorniczak (Poland)/Creative Commons

Published by Sourcebooks
1935 Brookdale RD, Naperville, IL 60563-2773
(630) 961-3900
sourcebooks.com

Cataloging-in-Publication Data is on file with the Library of Congress.

Printed and bound in the United States of America.
VP 10 9 8 7 6 5 4 3 2 1

To my mother,

my fiercest advocate and greatest encourager,

whose grace, love, and wisdom guided

me through my first period and continues

to guide me every day of my life.

Contents

Introduction

"There's Blood"

"There's blood," I whispered. My mom's eyes widened as she slowly processed my words. Without alerting my father, brother, or sisters, she silently slipped into the bathroom after me.

I immediately felt both relief and pride. I was relieved to check off what felt like another task on my to-do list and proud that I'd done exactly as I was told.

Several months before, my mother had held my shoulders and firmly stated, "If you ever see blood when you use the restroom, you need to let me know *immediately*."

Although her face was soft, the nervous shifting of her eyes and her forced smile betrayed her worry. But I had no clue what she could be worried about. As far as I had gathered, blood could be totally normal at my age. Also, the way she said "immediately" suggested that there was some sort of consequence for delay. My life's goal was to avoid all unnecessary or unpleasant consequences.

Back then, I was a confident, straight A student who felt like the only barrier to my imminent success was my age. My perfectionism in school was the direct result of undiagnosed anxiety and a need to seek external validation as a textbook middle child.

In all honesty, I wasn't *actually* the middle child in my home. I was the third of four children. My brother was seventeen, my older sister was fourteen, I was thirteen, and my little sister was nine. Even so, I justified my middle child title by using simple math. I was the person closest to the mean and median age. Furthermore, there was no other title up for grabs. My brother was the oldest child and only boy. My older sister was the oldest girl. And my younger sister was the youngest girl and youngest child. "Second girl" and "third child" were just unacceptable.

My older sister started her period two years before I did when she was in seventh grade. I was aware of what was happening but hadn't really asked any questions. I kind of hated asking questions. I preferred to read about topics or figure things out myself. I'm not certain why I felt that way, but I suspect it had something to do with the way my older siblings would poke fun at me when I asked questions like "Is Montana a state?" at the age of five or anything else totally appropriate for my age. Needless to say, I planned to figure out periods on my own.

My plan took a curveball one afternoon in seventh-grade health class. It wasn't a true health class but more like a brief talk on periods led by my social studies teacher. I was seated in the front row, silently doubting my teacher's qualifications for discussing the topic, when she shared some heavy-hitting information.

"Periods can last up to seven days," she said.

I asked her to repeat the statement for clarification. When she said it again, I tried to hide my shock, but my peers quickly concluded that the only explanation for my visible distress was that I'd never had a period. I was mortified. After the class ended, a much taller and much more developed girl came up to me in the hallway and said, "You know doctors can give you a shot to help you start, right?"

Ironically, I did not know that.

Everyone knew that my father was one of the few ob-gyns in town, but he'd never mentioned periods to me, let alone had a conversation with me about them. And there I was, staring into the tiny magnetic mirror in my locker, questioning whether I needed medical intervention. I was pissed. I wasn't allowed to say "pissed," but even I knew that was the only word to accurately describe my growing rage. I was pissed at every adult in my life, especially the Southern women I grew up around who had always used the ambiguous "time of the month" phrase, leaving me to believe periods lasted, at max, one day. I went to the school library to look for reliable resources on the matter and got nowhere. I waited for the rest of seventh grade for a period that didn't come.

So when my mom grabbed my shoulders and instructed me to tell her if I ever saw blood, I was encouraged. My mom, the womanliest woman I knew, still had faith that my body could develop normally. I had a supporter and a confidant. I needed only to let her know when the time came.

Despite my personal preference to know as much information as possible beforehand, I concluded that a pre-period discussion must have been optional. And my mom had opted out.

I wasn't completely in the dark about puberty though. I knew to wash my face to decrease acne and to wear deodorant to avoid odor. I'd also reluctantly let my cousin teach me how to shave under my arms. Unfortunately, my guidance had been reactive in nature, leading me to associate most of these new hygiene practices with ways to avoid embarrassment or shame. I carried over the same association when it was time to learn about my period.

Now my mom looked in the toilet bowl and said, "Yep. You've started your period."

There was no celebration or grief, just acknowledgment. And I preferred it that way. I hated it when people celebrated normal things. I can't begin to express how annoyed I was at my fifth-grade graduation. *All this just to head to sixth grade?!*

Even so, I was excited to have expert confirmation. My body had finally come through for me!

Then I remembered that today was the day the entire family was heading to the pool. As it was for most kids my age, swimming was the highlight of my summer. There was nothing better than jumping into the pool, doing flips underwater, and challenging my siblings to handstand contests. I always stayed in the water as long as possible, my happiness growing with every new wrinkle on my fingers.

My mom let out a deep sigh, walked down the hall to her bedroom, and returned with a tampon. "If you want to swim today, you'll have to use one of these," she said.

At that time, I knew nothing about tampon taboos, controversies, or fears. I only knew that I would still be able to swim if I used one. So I did. It wasn't weird, painful, or difficult. I had a wonderful day at the pool with my family and remain grateful to my mom for her guidance.

The detailed period talk that I was expecting never happened, however. Instead, my mom gave me a short list of rules.

1. Never wear tampons longer than eight hours, and never sleep in them.
2. Always wrap used period products in toilet paper before throwing them away.
3. Dispose of pads and tampons in a personal trash bag during your period, and then personally place that bag in the large trash bin in the garage.
4. No one should ever know that you're on your period.

I felt like I'd made it into a secret order of menstruators and assumed the rules were nonnegotiable and universally applied. I lived my life accordingly, hiding my period with diligence and skill until my mother passed away when I was twenty-nine.

As I got older, I gained a new appreciation for how progressive my mom was to teach me how to use a tampon with my first period. I also began to have better ideas about why she seemed worried about me starting my period and why she made sure to be the first to know when I did.

My mom exemplified grace, understanding, open-mindedness, and love. She was brilliant, accomplished, and known for her kindness. While she certainly subscribed to some of the old-school standards of femininity, she also planted deep seeds of self-love, courage, and confidence within me and my sisters. She is the reason that I smile when I am underestimated and speak up when I am disrespected. I could not have had a better mom, but I could have had a better period education.

In my career as a gynecologist for adolescents, I've had the unique privilege of observing hundreds of parent-child pairs, and I've noted some key truths over the years. There is a strong association between the puberty and period experiences of my patients and their parents' attitudes and beliefs around menstruation. Dads who associate menstruation with something negative or dirty often distance themselves, leaving their former "daddy's girls" feeling abandoned. Parents who regret their own history of early sexual activity tend to hyperfocus on policing their teen's relationships, punishing them for normal sexual exploration. Moms who were objectified due to early breast development or their curvier figures often preach clothing standards that are overly modest and repressive, making their child feel unworthy of being seen.

I never got a chance to ask my mom why she approached periods the way she did. I don't know what events or experiences influenced her style of parenting or how she decided the best way to guide her three daughters through the process. I imagine that her views were shaped in a time when femininity and discretion were equally valued. She probably didn't fear tampons because she did her own research and learned how to use them safely and responsibly. She may have been embarrassed once or twice by someone seeing a soiled pad or tampon in the family garbage, so she taught a double measure of caution related to product disposal. Although I've accepted the truth that I'll never know her reasons, my curiosity on the matter remains.

The interest continued throughout my years of practice as I observed several prevailing parenting styles. While I would often try to address overt displays of projection and policing, it wasn't always the right place, and there was never enough time to have the kinds of nuanced discussions I thought would truly make a difference. I kept saying to myself, *I wish these parents knew how much damage they are causing by making their children feel ashamed of their bodies. I wish they knew how impactful they could be in their children's overall experience of puberty and periods.* Wishing turned into writing, and writing made way for this book.

As a parent or someone who cares for children, you don't have to be an expert on periods, but it is your responsibility to guide your child safely and appropriately through this impactful transition. This stage of their development is critically important and creates the foundation for their relationship with themselves and with others. It is not your chance at a puberty redo, and your past is not automatically their future. Every child deserves their own puberty and period experience. Your job is simply to be there to guide them.

In this book, I'll demonstrate the imperative of intentional parenting. I'll discuss the leading ways in which parents negatively impact their children's puberty experience and explore why so many of them resort to the same outdated attitudes and methods. I'll then explain the fundamentals of puberty and periods with medical accuracy, honesty, and modern-day application. Finally, I'll share my recommendations for healthy parenting practices that reframe the puberty and early period years as a time for shared learning, partnership, and growth.

With this book, you *will* be able to parent differently. You *will* break generational cycles of shame and embarrassment around puberty and periods. You *will* make things better for your child. Let's start a revolution.

1

Opting Out Is Not an Option

The small room was poorly ventilated and getting hotter with each passing second, but I was still trying to process what I'd just been told. "Let's just check it again," I said.

"I already did," she replied. "Believe me, it is positive."

I was standing with my nurse in the tiny utility closet that also served as our makeshift lab. We were whispering, careful not to be overheard.

It wasn't that I didn't believe her. She was excellent at her job and knew our rule: *If a pregnancy test is ever positive, check it again.* I was hesitating because this had never happened since I had started practicing as an adolescent gynecologist.

I'd only been in practice for about a year, but I was finally getting into a good groove. I had an incredible team that I trusted, and we had an efficient, effective system to treat our patients. Inspired by my many years of training, I'd implemented protocols to maximize efficiency, minimize error, and improve patient experience. One such protocol was related to urine testing. I'd been trained to always collect urine from new patients, especially those requesting contraceptive services. With just one urine sample, we could test for bladder infections, sexually transmitted infections (STIs), and pregnancy. Our process was to have this done at the beginning of the visit for two reasons. The first was because adolescents are notoriously terrible at providing urine samples. Something about asking them to pee on command makes their hearts race and their bladders clench up. Seriously, entire clinic schedules have been delayed just because we had to wait a half hour for a few drops of pee. If it was going to take two or three tries to get a sample, I preferred we start early. Secondly, this allowed us to run any necessary testing on the urine while simultaneously gathering past medical history and completing physical exams.

This new patient was no different. She was twelve years old and accompanied by her mom for a contraceptive counseling visit, so a urine sample was promptly collected on arrival, along with a consent form for testing. Thankfully, she had no trouble peeing.

My initial encounter with her and her mother was unremarkable. She reported that her daughter had been asking to get on birth control for a while, and she was finally able to make time to bring her in. Her mom wasn't a woman of many words, but somehow her daughter spoke even less. It was such a struggle getting them to engage with me that I was relieved when my nurse called me out to review the testing results.

I stared at the first set of double lines and then at the second before finally accepting the facts. This patient was pregnant. There was no point in wishing otherwise. And I was going to have to tell her. I sighed and returned to her room, this time asking her mother to step out.

"Can you tell me more about why you want to be put on birth control?" I asked.

"I just do," she answered flatly.

"And you don't have any period concerns? You just need to prevent pregnancy, is that right?" I asked.

"Yes."

"Have you already begun to have sex or just thinking about it?" I pushed, looking for more context.

No response.

"Are you dating anyone currently?"

She frowned.

"Listen, I know you just met me, and you may not feel like you can trust me. Honestly, that makes sense. But I've got to tell you something that's serious, and we're going to need to work together to figure out what comes next."

Silence.

I sighed. "We tested your urine today when you came in, and it shows that you're pregnant," I said.

I watched as she grasped the gravity of my words. Her eyelids began to flutter, and fear flickered behind her dark eyes. Her tough exterior immediately crumbled, revealing what had always been a scared twelve-year-old girl. When she started to cry, I gathered her small frame in my arms. I hugged her while her tears soaked the shoulder of my white coat until she composed herself enough to pull away. When she did, I realized I'd been crying too.

I stepped out briefly while she shared the news with her mom. I'd offered to stay or even tell her mom for her, but she preferred to tell her herself.

When I returned to the room several minutes later, her mom looked stunned. I sat silently, holding space for the many emotions that lingered, until her mom quietly asked, "What do we do?"

I learned that she was a single mom who worked long hours. So when the school bus dropped her daughter off each day, she was instructed to go home and stay there. She could help herself to food in the fridge and complete her homework, but she wasn't allowed to leave, and she wasn't allowed have anyone over. It turns out a boy who lived in her neighborhood noticed her and began to hang around. He asked to hang out with her while her mom was gone and, at some point, convinced her to have sex with him. She didn't even know what sex was until she did it for the first time. Even then, she wasn't sure. She wasn't sure how many times it had happened and didn't feel like she had been forced. She enjoyed the company and just thought he liked her. It had been going on for several weeks, and her mom was completely unaware.

The mom had told her daughter to stay away from boys but had never talked to her about sex. When the girl started her period last year, her mom told her to use pads but never talked with her about how she could possibly get pregnant. She had never discussed what a healthy relationship looked like or how some people weren't safe to be around, even other kids. But that's because she didn't think she needed to. Her daughter hadn't even shown interest in dating. She just didn't know how this could have happened.

I counseled them on their options and gave them a list of providers and clinics. When I chose to specialize in pediatric and adolescent gynecology, I stopped practicing obstetrics to focus on this area of need. A gynecologist is a physician who provides care for conditions that affect the female reproductive organs. A pediatric and adolescent gynecologist is one who is specially trained in the care of children and adolescents. I provided gynecology care to my patients but no longer delivered babies or managed pregnancies.

Because I didn't see pregnant patients in my practice, I couldn't continue caring for her until after her pregnancy. For months after their visit, I wondered what happened to her and what choice she made. I also thought of her mother often. She was a good mom who was working hard to provide for her child. She did her best to keep her daughter safe while she was away. She thought school would handle the sex talk or her daughter would learn on her own. She felt like she had enough on her plate, and this was something she could forgo. Someone else would do it. Somehow, it would get done. But it didn't get done. Her daughter's naivety was exploited, and she had to experience one of the toughest and most avoidable lessons of her life.

While it is unfair to say that her mother is to blame, if she could go back in time, I'm sure she would've done things differently. If she could, I believe she would've made the time to teach her daughter the things that might have protected her. She would have chosen an awkward and uncomfortable conversation over this devastating and traumatizing consequence. She wouldn't have opted out.

IIIIIIIIIIIII

"Opting out" is a term commonly used to describe the act of declining what is standard or recommended. For example, it is standard that parents are responsible for guiding and teaching their children the foundational matters of life that will allow them to become safe, healthy, productive, and fulfilled adults. Because puberty is the transition from physiological childhood to adulthood, it requires acknowledgment of and instruction on topics that are related to pubertal events but can also be applied to practices and experiences of adulthood. The potentially sensitive and stressful nature of these topics can understandably trigger avoidance from parents for many reasons, including their own past trauma or uncertainty about where to start. Moreover, with the addition of personal values, cultural influences, and religion, the specifics on how, when, and where to best provide information related to puberty and sexual development are heavily debated.

Many parents still believe their child will be taught the basics about their changing body in school. They recall an outdated, romanticized scene where students are separated by gender and provided an educational overview on parts of the body, how they work, and how they should care for them. This hypothetical class is effective, brief, noncontroversial, and unbiased. There's no hidden agenda, and no one is offended, because it promotes health and wellness and nothing more. It doesn't need to be revisited and doesn't offer remediations because each student leaves fully prepared to manage puberty, hormones, perspiration, and peer pressure. And for that, parents are both thankful and relieved.

The trouble is this class doesn't exist, and it never has.

Health education, due to its unavoidable and necessary inclusion of sexual health topics, has never been without controversy. Sex ed classes have occurred in U.S. public schools since the 1960s.[1] Opposition and legal challenges to these classes have occurred for nearly as long. While some of these sex ed programs balance counseling on STI and pregnancy prevention with guidance on positive communication and relationships, other programs promote a moral imperative of sexual purity with abstinence-only instruction. These prevailing extremes center around the previously heated discussion on whether discussing sex with adolescents leads to greater sexual exploration and activity. Spoiler: It does not. Even so, for decades, groups of parents have condemned school-based sex ed courses for undermining their right to parent their children as they see fit.

This was such a significant concern that in 1971, parents in the town of Hamden, Connecticut, organized to obtain a temporary injunction of their local school's mandatory health education course. They specifically cited the course's inclusion of the following topics in their complaint: reproduction, hygiene, family life, and growth. They claimed that the teaching of this course in public school was a violation of their constitutional right to free exercise of religion, meaning they felt that this type of information hindered their ability to raise their children with the religious views and values that they preferred. The court ultimately upheld the course as constitutional, but the battle between parental preferences and public education policy is a long-standing and ongoing one.[2]

But not all parents oppose sex ed in school. In fact, parental support for sex education in public schools increased from 78 percent in the 1970s to 90 percent in 2012.[3] More recent studies show that most parents remain in favor of sex education. A 2021 survey of parents of school-aged children in Minnesota showed that 90 percent were in support of comprehensive sex education.[4] A 2022 meta-analysis of U.S.-based studies found that 90 percent of parents supported sex education.[5] A study published in 2025 from a national U.S. sample showed that 95 percent of parents felt topics such as transmission of STIs and healthy relationships were important and should be taught in school-based sex education.[6]

Despite widespread parental support, the provision of formal sex ed has declined over the past three decades. Only thirty-six states and the District of Columbia require sex education to be taught in schools. Even fewer require the inclusion of contraception in the course material or that the information provided be medically accurate. When states do require medical accuracy, they don't often describe what that means.[7] A 2022 study concluded that "young people in the U.S. today are less likely to receive sex education on key topics needed to protect their sexual health than they were twenty-five years ago."[8] With the current political climate, the number of kids receiving medically accurate, science-based sexual education in their public schools will only decline.

There's a growing trend, frequently initiated by political figures, of limiting how and when schools are allowed to teach sex ed. In 2022, Florida Governor Ron DeSantis signed what many referred to as the "Don't Say Gay" law. It banned public-school teachers from providing classroom instruction on sexual orientation or gender identity. It banned books that discussed sexuality and gender from the public-school libraries as well. The law specifically prohibited the discussion of these topics in kindergarten through third grade, citing an effort to allow parents to determine when and how to introduce LGBTQ+ topics to their children. Moreover, it gave parents the option to sue the school district if the new policy were to be violated. During a press conference, DeSantis said teaching kindergarteners that "they can be whatever they want to be" was "inappropriate" for children.[9] The law doesn't consider that students may begin to have questions and start exploring gender identity as young as age three or four. It doesn't make exception for a student who may have same-sex parents, a nonbinary sibling, or a relative who is transgender. It effectively bans the acknowledgment of LGBTQ+ identity, history, and culture until the arbitrary and nonevidence-based level of maturity marked by fourth grade.

If this doesn't bother you, please know that DeSantis didn't stop there. In 2023, he signed into law what critics called the "Don't

Say Period" bill. This law was an expansion of the "Don't Say Gay" law, not just limiting the use of preferred pronouns and classroom instruction on gender identity but also restricting instruction on reproductive health. The law restricted sexual and health education in grades K–12. In addition to requiring teachers of all grades to get approval of all materials used in sex ed, the law also prevents the discussion of human sexuality, STIs, and other related subjects before sixth grade. Related subjects included menstruation.[10]

The irony is that the average student is eleven years old when they enter sixth grade, and they turn twelve at some point during the school year. The average age of first period is also twelve, which means that half of children who menstruate will get their period before receiving any kind of formal instruction about human sexuality in school. Additionally, age of puberty onset and first period has been trending younger and younger for the past few decades. Most female students enter puberty before sixth grade, and at least half of them begin menstruation before then. This means many students will have already had to manage their period within the school setting, all while not being able to learn about it there. It almost guarantees increased stigma and shame for those students—an unfair and preventable harm.

A darker irony is that the average age that kids get their first smartphone is eleven. Seventy-five percent of kids have phones by age twelve.[11] This normalized and often necessary milestone of adolescent independence comes with a drastic increase in access to information. Misinformation and disinformation are propelled to large audiences through social media platforms. Despite increased regulations, the rapid spread of this content often outpaces new policy geared toward prevention. In addition to exposure to images that can promote excessive body comparison and negative self-image, smartphones give tweens and teens nearly constant access to websites and platforms with sexually explicit and pornographic content.

Adolescent pornography use has steadily increased over the last several years, with the age of first exposure getting younger. Approximately 70 percent of U.S. adolescents report exposure to online pornography. Some 54 percent reported seeing porn by age thirteen, with 15 percent saying they saw porn for the first time before age eleven.[12] Exposure to pornography may lead to higher risk sexual behaviors as well as set unrealistic expectations, beliefs, and attitudes around sex. These attitudes often minimize the importance of consent, encourage violence, and overemphasize appearance. Despite the well-known harms of porn exposure, many young people are turning to porn as a place to learn about sexuality. Experts describe porn as the new replacement for sex ed, with 45 percent of teens agreeing that online pornography gives helpful information about sex.[13]

But this book isn't about sex. It is about puberty and periods, right?

Yes and no.

This book is about providing children with the information, resources, and safety to manage their changing bodies, emotions, and relationships with confidence and agency. It is about honoring who our children are and loving them so fiercely that when given the option, they choose to love themselves and spend time with those who love them too. It is about giving them a foundation so solid it withstands the storms of adolescence and carries them through to adulthood. It is sex education because it is reproductive health education, and reproductive health education is life education.

Sex education as we know it is declining largely due to political attacks on when, how, and what schools can teach. Our kids are being exposed to misinformation, disinformation, and pornographic content, influencing their attitudes and beliefs around body image and intimacy. Periods are starting younger, and educational resources are getting banned. So what do we do?

I propose a parent-led revolution.

We already know that parents are a critical influence on their child's sexual and reproductive health. Studies show that parents have a stronger impact on their children's health when family conversations about sex and sexuality are ongoing. The American Academy of Pediatrics (AAP) recommends that parents begin having open and honest conversations about sexuality in early childhood. Early childhood is defined as the years from birth through age eight. The AAP recommends parents have these conversations in a repeated and reciprocal fashion. By doing this, parents have numerous opportunities to clarify, reaffirm, and reinforce the values, skills, and standards they want to teach their children. These frequent and early conversations also allow kids to ask questions as they learn more and challenges arise. Parental openness encourages kids to put into practice what they've learned and seek help if they encounter unexpected or unintended outcomes in their social and sexual lives. This is why all physician groups and health organizations that support comprehensive sex education also advocate for parents to be their children's primary sexuality educators.

To start open discussions early, they must be approached in a way that is relevant and age appropriate. This begins with discussing basic external anatomy during potty training that helps your child learn how to urinate, defecate, and clean themselves effectively. It then changes to differentiating between appropriate and inappropriate touch as they start to attend school and spend more time outside the home. And once puberty begins, appropriate guidance includes the accurate and open discussion of how and why their body is changing. The "why" is what lends itself to sexual health education. It is only with a solid foundation and understanding of puberty and periods that essential sexual health education can be applied. And although this approach would help to prevent the patient scenario I shared earlier, this isn't something I promote for my benefit as an adolescent gynecologist. Children genuinely want to learn this information. In fact, it is too often the parents and adults in their lives who are holding them back from the knowledge they crave.

A 2023 national survey of menstruating teens and menstruating adults revealed that adults are less likely to feel comfortable talking and communicating about periods, and teens have noticed.

Seventy-two percent of teens reported that they are more comfortable than their parents' generation talking about menstruation.[14] As teens spend more time turning to online sources and talking with friends, parents are left out in the periphery, still grappling with their own shame, discomfort, and lack of information. And this isn't just an issue in the United States.

Parents all around the world are expected to provide sexual health guidance to their children, often without the necessary information to do so. A study of parents in Nepal revealed that 40 percent communicated with their adolescents about sexual and reproductive health, but only 30 percent had correct knowledge themselves about menstruation, hygiene, and sexual health topics. Parents who had the necessary knowledge and understanding of puberty were more likely to communicate with their children about it, showing that a lack of knowledge is a barrier to parental guidance and communication.[15]

But parents can learn! A study done in Ghana showed that even short-term training of parents on matters of reproductive and sexual health positively impacted their attitudes and knowledge. They found that when parents are given the resources to learn about adolescent development, decision-making, sexuality, and even contraception options, they are not only more knowledgeable, but they are also more likely to engage. They're more open to discussing these topics with their children as well as allowing them to use important and evidence-based protective measures like condoms or contraception if needed.[16]

As a parent or guardian, you are perfectly positioned to be the change necessary in the menstrual education and sexual health space. You want your child to live a happy and fulfilled life, not just in adulthood but also in their childhood. You understand how critical the pubertal years are and how impactful they can be to self-esteem, relationships, academics, athletics, and more. Puberty isn't just about body odor and acne; it is about the pivotal time in which your child begins the process of becoming the adult they will eventually be.

So if you grew up being embarrassed of your normal development and ashamed to discuss things like menstruation, cramps, or premenstrual syndrome (PMS), you now have the opportunity and obligation to make sure your child never feels that way.

There's no class, community program, or pamphlet that can ever replace the warmth, safety, and guidance of a loving parent. Your influence cannot be banned or legislated. No executive order can erase your child's unique soul or invalidate their authentic existence. It is time for parents to do what no one else can: protect and preserve the reproductive freedom of the next generation.

In the following chapters, I'll provide you with the tools and information to confidently and compassionately show up for your kids when they need you the most. They may not admit it or acknowledge it, but they will remember how it felt to have a parent who didn't pull away during puberty but leaned in closer instead. They will remember how you didn't react with anger or panic when they asked you about their reproductive or sexual health. They will remember the constant nature of your love and support in the chaos of adolescence.

The changes of puberty and periods are not ones that can generally be modified or controlled. They will come, often without permission or adequate warning. They will progress without consideration for your preparedness or personal preferences. They will likely offend your expectations and breach the limits of your comfort zone. But without your guidance through this transition, your child's self-esteem, physical health, emotional wellness, and safety are left up to chance. I beg you not to take that gamble.

Now is the time to uproot shame, stigma, and self-doubt and plant acceptance, understanding, agency, and power. Now is the time for you to opt in.

In this next chapter, we will begin to examine your beliefs, challenge your biases, and explore your pain. That's where the true revolution begins.

2

It Is Not About You...But It Is

One morning, I prepared to see a new patient for an unknown complaint. The day was slow, so I spent a few minutes speculating about what her needs could be. Period pain? Abnormal bleeding? Breast concerns? When my nurse interrupted my guessing game to deliver the visit intake form, my curiosity gave way to disappointment. Written in the blank next to "reason for today's visit" was "find out if sexually active." I sighed and began to mentally prepare to traverse challenging terrain that I'd navigated plenty of times before.

As I entered the exam room, I found a woman and a girl seated next to each other against the far wall. They'd appropriately left the small gray rolling stool and beige exam table on the opposite side of the room untouched. The woman, who appeared to be in her mid-thirties, was wearing a uniform that I recognized from a local grocery store. Because of the early time of day, I gathered she'd likely planned to head directly to work after the appointment concluded. The girl appeared to be in her early teens and was also wearing a uniform, this one from a local school. As she swung her legs in her seat with childlike focus, I was reminded that she was younger than her pubertal features made her look. She held her elbows and folded her shoulders inward. This was a posture characteristic of my patients who also used oversize shirts and jackets to conceal their growing chest. Despite their physical proximity to each other, the woman and the girl appeared to be miles apart mentally.

"Good morning," I said, breaking the silence with a smile.

My greeting was met with a nonverbal sound from the woman that somehow still effectively communicated that she found this morning to be anything but good.

I chose to stick with my script anyway.

"You must be Melody."

The girl nodded with a polite but fleeting smile.

I smiled back at her. "And who do you have with you today?"

"I'm her mom," the woman said, emphasizing her words with her shoulders instead of her hands as she seemingly refused to uncross her arms.

"Lovely," I replied. "And what brings you in to see me today?"

I asked that question as a point of strategy. Melody rolled her eyes and nodded her head toward her mother, confirming my assumption. She hadn't asked to be here. It was her mother who was looking for answers.

"I'm trying to find out if she's having *sex*, because I'm her *mother* and I *need* to know," she said, glaring at Melody.

Melody avoided her mom's glare and instead fixed her gaze over my right shoulder, staring blankly at the door. She looked angry and embarrassed but not surprised.

It was clear to me that her mother was on a mission to confirm her own suspicions. From the look of it, she felt quite confident in them too.

"Okay. Tell me more about that," I said.

This is my favorite phrase to use in situations like this. In my years of training, I found that many of the doctors I worked with and learned from operated almost entirely on their own assumptions. Full clinic visits and complete care plans were determined before entering the room, before meeting the person behind the concern, and before the humanity of that person could ever be fully considered. I vowed to never practice that way. Even if the visits took longer, I wanted to understand where my patients were coming from before offering recommendations. So I let Melody's mom speak.

Her mom told a story I knew very well. Melody's body was changing, and her attitude was too. She was getting looks from guys, flirting with boys, and people around town were saying she had a boyfriend. Her mom was no fool. In fact, her mom hadn't been too different herself. Her body developed earlier than the other girls in her grade, and she started having sex at a young age. She was still a teen when she gave birth to Melody. Because she didn't want the same thing for Melody, she decided she wasn't about to let her daughter get one over on her. She was convinced that Melody was sexually active, and she'd come to me to confirm what she thought she already knew.

I took this all in, nodding to confirm my comprehension. But I still needed to know a little bit more.

"So what exactly are you looking for me to do today?" I asked.

"I want you to do the test...where you look at her hymen," she said. "I tried to look, but I couldn't see."

I took a deep breath in, as I'd trained myself to do, and silently commanded my face to stay neutral. I had to hide any signs of disapproval or judgment. Judgment in a sensitive patient encounter was like a death blow. It destroyed any chance of connection, reconciliation, or resolution. Even so, my stomach turned as I fought away the images that came to mind of a clumsy, intrusive, at-home hymen exam.

I took another deep inhale before speaking again, this time directly to her mom.

"I'm so happy you brought your daughter in to see me today, and I want to thank you for sharing your concerns with me. I can tell you really care about her, and you genuinely want her to be safe, especially at her age."

Melody's mom nodded in agreement.

"I want her to be safe too, because her safety is essential to her health, and her health is my priority. For that reason, I must let you both know that there's no test for virginity. Doctors can't tell by just looking at the hymen whether someone has had sex before, and doing an unnecessary exam like that can be uncomfortable and even traumatizing."

I waited to let that last statement sink in.

"So if I wanted to know if Melody was sexually active, I'd just ask her. But not so that I can report it back to you. I'd ask her to make sure she understood the risks and had the tools and resources to be safe and protected."

"So you won't do the test?"

"There is no test."

Despite her mother's disappointment, I was able to speak with Melody privately. She denied being sexually active and shared that she wasn't even dating. She was very aware of the risks of sex and had no intention of becoming a mother in her teens. She'd seen how hard it was on her own mom and how much regret her mom seemed to have. She didn't want to go through what her mom had experienced.

We talked about how she wanted to go to college out of state and study nursing. We also talked about how she loved to draw and wouldn't mind also studying art. At the conclusion of my talk with her, it was clear that her mom was projecting her own past trauma and mistakes onto her daughter. Melody was bright, ambitious, capable, and kind. Her mom had done a good job raising her on her own all these years. I wanted her to know that.

I went to the waiting room to try to speak with her mother again, but she was already gone. She'd told my receptionist to let Melody know she'd be waiting in the car. I never got to tell her how sorry I was that her early development made her feel so lost and ashamed. I never got to tell her how I understood that society often projects an adultification bias on young Black girls that can force them to feel like they need to grow up quicker. I didn't get to tell her how common it is for a child's puberty to trigger old feelings of insecurity and isolation. I didn't get to tell her that Melody had already learned a lot from her and wanted the same things for her life that she hoped for her to have. I didn't get to tell her there was still time to heal, repair, and positively support her daughter in these critical years of change.

IIIIIIIIIIIII

Depending on your past experiences, your child's puberty experience may trigger some old wounds. This is largely because these pivotal years correlate closely with the onset of negative scenarios, feelings, and conditions for many people. This includes everything from self-esteem issues to mental health conditions, bullying, objectification, embarrassment, assault, and more. They may be small, superficial abrasions or larger wounds that penetrate well beyond your first few layers of protection. Whether these wounds were caused by your own actions, the actions of others, or a combination of both, you may still feel pain.

Pain is a sensory experience that is meant to cause a response. It is one of the most important survival signals that our bodies can send to our brains because it communicates danger and prompts us to make modifications to bring about its relief. Pain is not just necessary, it is protective, because the unawareness of injury leaves us vulnerable to worse harm. So if it is necessary to feel pain, and the perception of that pain is not a choice, the choice then lies in how we respond to it.

It is well established that we respond to our experiences with emotions. The experience of pain, for example, can trigger emotions of fear, confusion, anger, or even sadness. Our emotions then inform our actions. In response to the emotions caused by pain, actions can vary from withdrawal to hypervigilance, projection, or even retaliation. Our actions then lead to consequences or results that ultimately form systems of beliefs.

The thing about beliefs is that they don't have to be based on fact. Beliefs are defined as something one accepts as true or a firmly held opinion or conviction. Consequently, they are as powerful as our commitment to them. When we are truly committed, our minds use our beliefs as daily guides. So when a similar experience presents itself, our beliefs activate a workflow of actions that we've consciously or subconsciously predetermined to be most protective or the best at avoiding the least desirable results. This applies to our social interactions, career opportunities, personal finances, and even our styles of parenting.

I shared with you that my mother responded to my first period with matter-of-fact awareness and shame-free counsel. As I began to see more and more adolescent patients, I realized that many parents didn't respond in this manner. It made me curious about their past experiences, their sources of pain, and the beliefs they'd formed to survive them.

I saw another teen who had been brought in by her father for a new patient visit years ago. Before I could get the visit started, the dad tried to leave the exam room.

"I'll leave you two to it then," he said, nearly leaping across the room and closing the door behind him.

I hadn't even finished introducing myself.

I followed him.

"Mr. Jones. Just a second, please!"

I explained to him that I typically begin the visit with the parent/guardian present and *then* ask them to step out.

"Oh, um…" He rubbed his head, and his eyes danced along the carpeted floor with palpable uneasiness. "I don't really have much to say about all that… Her mom couldn't make it…and…"

"I just need to ask about family history, a few things about home and school life, and then you'll be done," I assured him.

"I'd really rather not," he said apologetically.

I returned to the room where my patient, Rachel, was rolling her eyes.

"I knew he'd leave the first chance he got. He hates all this stuff."

"What stuff?" I asked. "Doctor's visits?"

"No." She laughed. "Woman stuff."

She shared that she'd been super close with her father growing up, but once she hit puberty and had to start wearing a training bra, her father became distant. When she started her period last year, her mom was on a work trip. She asked her dad what she should do, and he panicked before calling their female neighbor. The neighbor came over with a pack of pads and gave her a brief tutorial before returning home. She was mortified. Her dad's avoidant behavior hurt her feelings and made her resent her body and the changes she was experiencing. It didn't help that her periods were also terribly painful.

After speaking with Rachel, I decided to try to speak with her father again. I found him sitting in the waiting room, still visibly uncomfortable.

"I'm happy you were able to bring your daughter in today. Her periods are pretty rough and have been causing her a lot of pain. Were you aware of that?"

His face softened. "Oh, um, no, I wasn't. How bad are they?"

"They make her miss softball practice sometimes, and she occasionally has nausea and vomiting," I said.

"I thought she just didn't like playing ball anymore," he said.

"Nope, she loves it. She just can't always show up like she wants to when she's in pain. She also really misses you," I added.

"What do you mean? I haven't gone anywhere," he said.

"She feels like your relationship has been different ever since she started puberty and got her period. She feels like you don't talk to her the same, spend time with her, or help her with softball anymore."

He looked sincerely apologetic. "I didn't realize that. I guess I just didn't want to say the wrong thing or upset her."

"But she is upset. She's hurting, and she doesn't feel like she can talk to you about it. Why do you think she feels that way?"

I learned that Rachel's father had grown up in a community where there weren't many examples of men engaging with women in healthy and supportive ways. He knew how to navigate women as romantic partners, platonic friends, and respected colleagues, but the idea of talking to his daughter about puberty or periods caused him major distress. He was once a proud "girl dad," supporting her in softball, track, and debate team. But he just didn't know where he fit in during this transitional time. Because he didn't know what to do, he elected to keep his distance. Instead of stepping in as a capable and compassionate parent, he withdrew, leaving his daughter to feel abandoned and resentful of her normal development and growth.

Parental responses to puberty are not always just about pain. Sometimes it is embarrassment, insecurity, discomfort, or fear. Sometimes it is the overwhelming feeling of needing to offer guidance in a situation that you never experienced or in an area where you never excelled. Sometimes you've only been exposed to the "wrong way," so the "right way" feels inaccessible or too difficult to achieve. Regardless of your personal history, your task remains the same. As the responsible adult in your child's life, you are charged with being a present and informed help during their pubertal years.

I was preparing to see a twelve-year-old patient one morning when my nurse stopped me with a sticky note that read "Given name is Elizabeth. Goes by Devin."

"Noted," I said, nodding to her before folding the note into my pocket and opening the door to the room.

"You must be Devin," I said.

"Yes," Devin said, beaming.

"I'm Dr. Chambers, and my pronouns are she and her," I said.

"They/them," they responded.

We smiled at each other.

Devin's pleasant surprise was cut short by their mom.

"I still call her Lizzy," she said dismissively.

"Okay," I said, looking back at my patient. "What do you prefer?"

"Devin," they said softly.

"What brings you in today, Devin?" I asked.

Their mom answered, "She started her period last summer, but it is all over the place. We never know when it is coming, and it is just not normal."

"Do you track the periods in an app or on a calendar?" I asked.

"Yes," Devin's mom answered.

She showed me her phone, which showed a four-to-five-day period occurring every six to ten weeks, with periods beginning just ten months ago.

"Thank you," I said after adding the details to the chart.

We reviewed family history, medications, allergies, and all the other basic medical information. Then I asked to speak with Devin alone.

"Behave yourself, Lizzy," Devin's mom said before closing the door.

Devin nodded and then frowned as soon as the door shut.

"I hate when she calls me that, and she knows it," they grumbled.

"Tell me more," I said.

"I told her I want to go by Devin. Lizzy is too girly, and it is just not me."

"When did you start feeling this way?"

"I think fifth grade, but maybe fourth grade. But when she tried to make me wear a bra and stuff, it just got worse."

"So things got worse when your breasts started to develop?" I asked.

"I was binding, and she got mad," they added.

"You were using a breast binder?" I asked.

"Well, I found an ankle wrap and some tape, so I used that. And it worked, but I stopped a while ago."

"What made you stop?" I asked.

"I didn't want to get cancer," Devin explained.

I squinted my eyes. "I'm sorry, what?"

"Breast cancer," Devin clarified. "My mom said if I kept binding, it would give me breast cancer."

I went to find Devin's mom. I talked with her about Devin's irregular periods and how they were within normal expectations for someone who started having periods so recently. I also let her know to call or schedule an appointment if Devin's bleeding was ever too long or too heavy. Then I brought up the breast binding.

"Devin tells me you told them breast binding causes breast cancer. Can you tell me more about that?" I asked.

She initially looked confused but very quickly gave in. "Okay, I made that up to get her to stop, but she was ruining her breasts," she admitted.

I spent the next ten minutes talking with her about how Devin had expressed feeling less aligned with being a girl and how the preferred pronouns of they/them suggested that they might feel more nonbinary. The breast binding may mean that their growing breasts caused some amount of gender dysphoria. Instead of manufacturing false consequences of breast binding, it would be more helpful to explore the real safety and risks of binding. I noted that Devin's mother could help ensure that the binding was being done with clean and breathable material that wasn't too tight on Devin's skin. She could help find Devin a mental health provider who specializes in gender identity and adolescents. What Devin needed was support, healthy curiosity, and love—not lies.

Because they are a unique individual with unique needs, your child's puberty experience is not about you. It is not your chance at a redo. It is not about making them into who you think they should be. It is not your opportunity to exploit their vulnerability in order to advance your political, religious, or social agenda. It is about listening and loving them while they grow into and discover who they are.

In order to do this, you must first spend time identifying your wounds. Identify the ways that you have been injured as it relates to puberty, sexual health, identity, body image, reproductive health, and relationships. Work to connect these wounds to the specific beliefs you had to form in order to grow, survive, or just exist in your life. Examine where these beliefs fail to align with facts and where they rely entirely on personal conviction. Name the sociocultural practices, biases, and learned behaviors that have shaped what you believe. Be honest about whether your belief-based actions have encouraged or discouraged the full and authentic expression of yourself or others. Ask yourself who this behavior reminds you of and whether the relationship you have with that person is one you'd want your child to have with you.

When something in this book challenges you, isolate the belief that you are being drawn to confront, and spend time with it. Interrogate its origin, validity, benefits, and harms. Unpack and heal these areas with therapy, counseling, meditation, journaling, or whatever other practice is necessary and most effective. Finally, open your mind to learning new information. This is your opportunity to form new beliefs—ones that promote positive actions, yield improved results, reinforce your goals, and allow your child to be healthy, happy, and whole.

3

Unlearn the Negativity

She does this sometimes," my patient's mom said.

I took note of the girl doubled over in pain who, from my vantage point as I sat in the exam room, was just an overturned head of braids, lavender sweatpants, and sneakers. I frowned, expressing the sympathy I felt for her pain.

"Don't fall for it," her mom said. "She acts like she's dying every time she has a period. It is exhausting."

I sighed. I wondered if the mom had considered how much more exhausting it might be to be the one experiencing the pain rather than just witnessing it.

"You must be Sarah. Is that right?" I asked.

Her head of braids nodded affirmatively, still completely concealing her face.

"I can tell you're in pain, but do you think you could share with me exactly what you're feeling?" I asked.

She looked up to meet my eyes and assessed me in silence. I sat, unflinching, while she weighed my request. I hid my relief when she ultimately deemed me trustworthy enough to go through the trouble of describing her pain.

"It feels like I'm being stabbed and burned…down on the inside."

Her mom stifled a laugh as she shifted in her seat.

Sarah frowned at me, and her eyes began to fill with tears. She was careful not to look over at her mother for fear of losing her nerve. I encouraged her to continue with a nod.

"The pain gets so bad and so intense that it makes me feel like I'm going to throw up." She paused. "Sometimes I actually do."

"Does anything make it better?" I asked.

"I try to rest or use my heating pad. But those don't help much," she responded.

"Do any pain medicines help?"

This time, her mom answered. "I don't let her use pain medicine. I never take pain medicine for my period! The way I see it, periods are normal, and she'll never be able to handle them if she's taking medicine every time she has a little bit of pain. Women were made to have periods. If that's how God made us, then He gave us the ability to handle them too."

This time, I directed my question to the mom. "You think God wants Sarah to be in pain?" I asked.

She was taken aback. I don't think she'd taken the time to really think about it that way before.

"I didn't say that. But God doesn't give us more than we can bear," she countered.

"But doesn't God promote healing? And didn't He give us medicine?" I asked.

"Well, yes. I suppose He did."

"Then why would you not let your daughter use medicine to help relieve her pain?" I asked. "Periods are different for every person," I said. "Some people are blessed to have pain-free periods while others spend their entire period in the fetal position, praying for relief. Using God as your reason for not treating her pain won't just make your daughter resent her body and her religion. It will make her resent you as well."

In a patriarchal society that ignores women's pain, mild period pain is more socially acceptable. Some menstruators may take pride in being able to handle their pain and in turn shame those who don't manage periods with the same tolerance. Whether they justify this disapproval with religion, false narratives around strength, or unrealistic cultural expectations, it's still harmful. Sarah's mom believed that all periods are manageable so strongly that she was more willing to conclude that her own daughter had to be exaggerating her symptoms or complaining to gain attention than to examine the flaws of her own belief system.

For many, unlearning old beliefs can feel like running up a down escalator, swimming against the current, or sailing against the wind. Due to the emotional, intellectual, and societal resistance that comes with confronting ingrained beliefs, many people avoid unlearning entirely. This is understandable. It is far more comfortable to stay misinformed than to confront a truth that might leave you feeling confused, conflicted, or convicted. This is especially the case when dealing with topics strongly associated with stigma and shame, like puberty and sexuality.

To unlearn the negative beliefs associated with menstruation and puberty, you must first acknowledge the adverse impact that these beliefs may have. This can be difficult when the foundation of a belief is personal, familial, or cultural in nature. For example, if the person who first taught you to hide your period was your grandmother, rejecting the belief that periods should be hidden can feel like a rejection of her as well. If the Bible taught you periods were unclean, denial of such can feel like denial of one's faith too. A major barrier to unlearning is the inability to separate the invalid belief from its valid origin.

While reconciliation is a personal endeavor that must be executed in accordance with one's unique needs and values, there are some general approaches that can be useful. As it relates to teachings from older generations, I've found reconciliation with a simple contextual pardon: "They did the best they could with what they knew at the time." Because of the stigma around menstruation, many mothers and grandmothers were taught very little about their bodies. People in marginalized communities, like Black women in the United States, weren't guaranteed access to medical treatment or quality care even if they had the correct information about their bodies. In turn, they were found responsible for teaching subsequent generations about reproductive health, all while navigating their own health without sufficient guidance, education, support, or access. For this reason, among many others, they filled in the missing pieces with what they could, often resorting to speculation, partial theories, and conjectures. By considering this context, we can give grace to our mothers and foremothers while still holding fast to the moral mandate for betterment and change.

As it relates to faith, I've found the matter to be more complex. Religion has been a major contributor to the negative stigma around menstruation. In addition to the biblical text of Christianity, the religions of Judaism, Hinduism, Buddhism, and Islam all have texts that ascribe impurity to menstruation. They all reference some requirement for separation or isolation for menstruators. These impure and ritualistically unclean views have been present for centuries and have helped to worsen gender inequalities. In religious spaces, menstruating women may be forbidden from praying, entering a place of worship, eating with family, preparing food, or even living in the same home. These practices have been used to exclude women from leadership positions as well as from decision-making roles.

Cultural beliefs around menstruation vary greatly in imagination and creativity but run along the same negative themes. In Kerala, India, some people believe if a woman leaves a cloth soiled with period blood out and fails to clean it, a snake will encounter it and die. It won't die because it's poisoned, however; it will die by beating its head on a stone. While doing this, it will curse the woman. This mythical snake is credited for cursing women who are unable to bear children. This is such a deeply held belief that people go to snake temples to pray for childless couples so that the curse might be lifted.

In South Korea, there is a belief that menstruating women shouldn't sit on a broomstick, because if it comes in contact with their menstrual blood, it will turn into a broomstick monster, a dokkaebi. In Kenya, a common belief is you shouldn't enter the garden while on your period because if you do, the crops will dry up.[1]

These myths may seem extreme and unrealistic, but I've heard many similar myths directly from my patients and their parents. I've had patients who were taught to never swim on their period. They weren't sure if swimming would cause infections or make them infertile, but they just knew it wasn't safe to do so—rules without reason.

The presence of religious or cultural teachings or rules in children's lives is not inherently negative, of course. The unequal application of these rules to women and girls with a consequential burden of blame, however, is flawed. While men are given governing power, they are paradoxically deemed unable to control their own sexual impulses. Their self-control evidently teeters at the mercy of female appearance, proximity, or behavior. Consequently, women can somehow be blamed for the assault or abuse they suffered because an outfit or action meant they were "asking for it." But that's not how it has to be.

Before embarking on this journey of unlearning, it is important to reconcile your personal cultural and religious views with your parenting practices. If you don't, you risk your child taking note of inconsistencies in your logic and losing trust in your guidance. Additionally, your parenting approach may become disjointed and confusing, to both you and your child, as the religion or customs you preach clash with the realities of the life you live. You don't have to be able to explain everything, but try to tease out those beliefs that directly conflict with the goals you have for your child, how you hope they will show up in life, and how you'd want them to navigate their future.

When you're ready, let's explore several of the most common negative reproductive health beliefs. We've already touched on the stigma around periods and bleeding, so let's start our unlearning there.

Eight Myths to Unlearn About Puberty

Myth 1: Periods are dirty.

Period blood is often considered to be the dirtiest, grossest, most detestable form of blood there is. Whether it is a visibly soiled period product or a period stain on the back of a dress, public response can be as extreme as gasps of horror or as dramatic as attempts to suppress vomiting. But period blood isn't "dirty." Period bleeding is made up of a mixture of some blood, some uterine tissue, and vaginal fluid. It does not contain toxins, poisons, or impurities.

In fact, menstrual blood is similar to other types of blood, like that found flowing through the arteries and veins of your body. It is not more prone to causing illness or infections, and as with other forms of bodily fluid, its cleanliness depends primarily on the health, hygiene, and exposures of the individual. So where does this stigma come from?

While it certainly is a by-product of religious doctrine, there's also a nonreligious misconception that contributes to this belief—the myth that menstruation is a detoxing process.

The term "toxin" is frequently used in today's society, most often by celebrities and influencers with health-adjacent interests and brands. Despite the wide and variable use of the word, toxin has a simple definition. A toxin is a harmful or poisonous substance that can cause disease or illness. Far too many people believe that the uterus removes toxins from the body via menstruation when this is not the case. These people are often the ones who strongly oppose the use of hormonal contraception, citing its disruption of the natural menstrual cycle as a form of unnecessary harm.

While there are organs that primarily function to remove toxins from the body, the uterus is not one of them. The colon, kidneys, lungs, and even skin remove toxins, which is why failure, injury, or removal of them is life-threatening. When someone develops kidney failure, for example, without regular dialysis of their blood, a fatal buildup of toxins will occur. When the uterus is removed, however, one can continue to live a full life with no looming threat of toxin accumulation or death. This is because menstruation is the cyclical shedding of the uterine lining, not a crucial toxin removal process. The menstrual blood that flows out is just blood, not a dirtier, more dangerous form of blood.

The issue with this type of misconception is that it depicts menstruation as abnormal, undesirable, and even inappropriate. This negative perception tends to extend to the person with the period too. The resulting stigma effectively impacts nearly every aspect of a menstruator's life. It can limit social development, athletic participation, educational aspirations, career advancement, and even healthcare utilization. The harm in the belief that periods are dirty and the impact of actions based on that belief are profound limitations, fractured self-esteem, unrealized potential, and significant shame. It promotes the opposite of what a good parent would want for their child and damages the self-love required to navigate the many challenges of the world.

Myth 2: Period pain is normal.

While my primary mission has always been the normalization of menstruation, I feel I work just as hard trying to prevent the normalization of the abnormal. As a society, pain is generally understood to be undesirable and worthy of relief, but when pain is associated with the female body, this view shifts. Pain that would warrant medical attention in other contexts is often considered to be, in the case of menstruators, tolerable, acceptable, and appropriate. From pain associated with intrauterine device (IUD) insertion to the pain of childbirth, the urgency around relief diminishes as soon as someone suspects a female reproductive cause for the pain. This bias is impacted by and even perpetuated by menstruators too.

Because people with periods have been encouraged to discuss their bodily functions in whispers and hushed tones, major issues and concerns related to menstrual pain and discomfort have gone unaddressed for far too long. Due to the embarrassment and shame around menstruation, entire communities and families have suffered from treatable conditions and delayed diagnoses all because they felt they couldn't discuss and thereby acknowledge that they needed help. The hallmark of present stigma is absent conversation.

While some amount of discomfort during or before one's period is common (often in the abdomen, pelvis, or lower back), it does not mean that all period pain is normal. Normal means typical or expected. Menstruation is normal because it is typical and expected, specifically between the ages of twelve and fifty-one. But there is a point where normal period discomfort transitions squarely into abnormal period pain. Although it may not be typical, whether it is expected relies almost entirely on individual perspective and exposure. This is why regular and frequent discussion of periods is so important.

Without access to research studies or medical expertise that define what is normal and what is not among the entire population, even debilitating pain can be "expected" when your entire family and everyone who ever taught you about periods has undiagnosed endometriosis. Breast tenderness, nausea, and vomiting for the first one or two days of menstruation can seem "normal" when you and all your close friends have severe PMS. Constipation, frequent urination, and pelvic pressure can feel like they should be manageable when your sisters and cousins all have fibroids.

It is not enough to speak with or compare yourself to your small circle of friends, family, coworkers, or teammates. Widespread dialogue across multiple generations and communities along with medical experts and researchers is necessary for the accurate understanding of normal and abnormal period pain.

Up to 90 percent of people with periods will experience some sort of pain or discomfort with menstruation.[2] Mild period pain is usually improved with exercise, heat therapy, or over-the-counter pain medication like nonsteroidal anti-inflammatory drugs (NSAIDs). This type of pain often occurs without an underlying cause and is secondary to the physiological rise in inflammatory chemicals that occurs at the beginning of menstruation. While this type of pain doesn't have an abnormal cause and could be considered typical or expected, it is still appropriate to treat it in order to achieve relief.

Pain is considered abnormal when it doesn't respond to the above interventions or when it severely impacts one's daily activities. That means if you can't attend school or work due to period pain, it's not normal. If you can't participate in athletics or your hobbies, it's not normal. If your pain is so severe that you develop nausea and vomiting, it's not normal. It doesn't matter if everyone in your family has these same symptoms. It doesn't matter that your coach or teacher doesn't mind monthly absences. If your pain is persistent or severe, it is not normal, and you are deserving of medical evaluation and treatment.

The obvious harm of normalizing abnormal pain is unnecessary suffering. The less obvious harm is found in what that suffering teaches us, especially at a young age. It teaches us that periods are a painful experience that we will be subjected to for the greater part of our lives. It teaches us not to discuss our period pain because there's no option for relief. It teaches us to avoid sports, to not pursue the promotion, and to forfeit the competition. The helplessness, hopelessness, and insecurity that follow teach us to resent periods and perpetuate the very stigma that we've fallen victim to.

Myth 3: Tampon use = sexual activity.

The purpose of a tampon is simply to absorb period flow within the vaginal cavity. By doing this internally instead of externally, it can offer improved comfort and better leak protection, especially for those participating in sports or water activities. As noncontroversial as that sounds, when discussed in certain communities and in relation to young menstruators, tampons can be quite polarizing.

One of the primary issues that many people have with tampon use is the misconception that familiarity with the vulva and insertion of a menstrual product inevitably promotes sexual exploration and eventual promiscuity. There is no research to support this, and the mere idea betrays the influence of a concerning system of beliefs.

First, it suggests that a person with a period is incapable of understanding their anatomy without associating it with sexual intercourse. This is an insulting school of thought that seeks to reduce menstruators to carnal and primitive beings instead of free-thinking people with agency, depth, and self-control. It further suggests that the use of a small absorbent menstrual product could bring about such an overwhelming desire for sexual pleasure that it might override the decision-making standards and values that have been instilled in a person for a decade or more. As harmful as this misconception is, you can ask any person who has ever used a tampon, and the last thing they would say it offers would be pleasure.

Another misconception is that tampons can only be used by someone who has already had penetrative sexual intercourse. This myth is based on the false belief that you cannot use a tampon unless your hymen has been broken, an event that is too often believed to be the hallmark of sexual activity. Research has shown that the appearance of the hymen is not a reliable predictor of sexual activity.[3] Furthermore, the appropriate use of tampons does not typically injure or change the hymen. A normal hymen is patent, or open. It will allow period blood to flow out and for a tampon to be inserted.

The harm perpetuated by a myth like this can be significant. The most common harm is when family members, typically parents or even aunts or uncles, falsely equate tampon use with sexual activity and go to extremes to inflict punishment on young menstruators for using them. Teens and children have been beaten, injured, and even killed because of this. In my practice, I heard a woman threaten to kick her granddaughter out of her home if she ever used tampons. These are the preventable and often unspoken consequences of reproductive health myths. Unlearning this myth is often followed by a moral mandate to advocate for young menstruators who desire to use tampons but fear the responses of those around them.

Myth 4: Getting your period makes you a woman.

This misconception has a more subtle negative impact than some others and is best explained through a series of definitions. It is generally agreed on that a girl is a female child, and a woman is a female adult. The difference between the two is largely age or maturity. Puberty is the physiological process by which a person changes from having more of a childlike body to more of an adultlike body. It is also defined as the process by which a child reaches sexual maturity or becomes capable of reproducing. Adolescence is the phase in which a child transitions to being an adult.

If we can agree on these basic definitions, we can also agree that adults don't go through puberty; children or adolescents do. An adult doesn't get their first period; a child or adolescent does. The first period may signal a newfound capability of reproduction, but it does not and should not signal the sudden onset of adulthood. Furthermore, it isn't the instantaneous end of childhood.

The reality is that some children start breast development at the age of seven or eight. Some get their first period at the age of nine. A nine-year-old isn't a woman. Even a pregnant nine-year-old is still a child. Equating the first period with the sudden onset of womanhood sends a very specific message to your child or adolescent. It tells them that their childhood, their time for continued nurturing, guidance, mercy, and protection, is over. It can give rise to feelings of abandonment, confusion, and insecurity.

Due to the significance and variety of changes taking place in their mind and body all at once, your child actually needs you the most during their pubertal transition. The hormonal shifts, mood swings, increased body hair, new acne, odors, and bodily fluids all warrant greater parental involvement and reassurance, not withdrawal and neglect. This isn't the time for unbridled independence. It is the perfect time for gentle supervision, measured responsibility, and collaborative learning.

Myth 5: Your child caused their early puberty.

Because puberty is so strongly and inappropriately associated with sexuality, there are some people who believe that early puberty occurs because of inappropriate sexual thoughts or behaviors. In some communities, early breast development may draw negative attention and whispered accusations of improper relationships. In some households, the initial narrowing of the waist and widening of the hips can induce reprimands and even punishment. In the most extreme scenarios, adolescents have been fatally harmed by family members who discovered their first period and felt it to be too soon.

The fact is that puberty is brought on by fairly complex signaling in the brain and typically begins anytime between the ages of eight and thirteen for biologically female children. To start, a wavelike release of gonadotropin-releasing hormone from one area of the brain stimulates the release of a luteinizing hormone

(LH) and follicle-stimulating hormone from another part of the brain. These hormones then activate the ovaries to produce estrogen and progesterone, leading to the physical changes that we recognize and associate with puberty in females. While environmental factors, like exposure to certain chemicals, diet, and obesity, can affect the timing of puberty, pubertal onset is primarily influenced by genetic causes. This means the primary influence on when puberty begins is inherited and at play well before the first physical change is noted. While this doesn't mean there is nothing that can be done to influence pubertal timing, it does mean that there's nothing your child or teen can do in terms of their behavior to cause it to start early.

It is worth noting that early puberty, or puberty beginning before the age of eight, isn't a completely benign process. It is associated with several potential physical, mental, and social issues. Even though genetics aren't modifiable, some nutritional and environmental influences are. Because children and teens don't usually control their environmental exposures, diets, or upbringings, this responsibility falls squarely on the adults in their lives, with the window of opportunity starting much earlier than many people realize.

Longer durations of breastfeeding, for example, are associated with reduced risk of early first period. Higher intake of plant-based protein in childhood as opposed to animal-based protein is also associated with later pubertal onset. A diet rich in fiber can also be protective against early puberty, along with adequate sleep and regular physical activity. If you're concerned about early puberty, there are several ways to potentially mitigate your child's risk through lifestyle choices. Once puberty begins, however, the appropriate response is support, guidance, and the involvement of medical professionals as needed.[4]

The early onset of pubertal changes can trigger emotions of alarm, confusion, or concern for parents and children, but it is never appropriate to blame or shame the affected child. Misplaced blame can cause significant damage to their self-esteem, interpersonal relationships, and overall mental health. It can teach your child to hide their body changes and health concerns from you. It can teach them that their body is broken or damaged. It can make them vulnerable to praise and attention from predatory parties who seek to exploit, abuse, or harm them. Puberty isn't a time to distance yourself from your child; it is a mandate to draw nearer.

Myth 6: Virginity is a medical diagnosis.

There are many communities around the world that still attach pride or value to virginity, or the state of never having engaged in sexual activity. There are countless flaws in this cultural value, but the most obvious one is the disproportionate application to women and girls. This custom is so common that in my practice as a pediatric and adolescent gynecologist, I have had parents request on numerous occasions that I evaluate or confirm their child or daughter's virginity status. I always decline, not only because it is absurd but also because it is not possible. Virginity is not a medical diagnosis, and there's no test for it.

Virginity as a status is determined by personal, social, cultural, and religious standards or beliefs. Despite what many people believe, there is no virginity exam or test. Any reports or accounts of a virginity exam are likely referring to an examination of the hymen. The hymen is a thin, fibrous tissue bridge located at the opening of the vagina. Examination of the hymen, however, is not a reliable way to determine whether sexual activity has occurred. It is not even a reliable way to determine whether abuse has occurred, a major limitation in the pursuit of justice for children who are victims of sexual abuse.[5]

The false belief that virginity can be confirmed or tested for by a medical provider is a dangerous one. It places pressure on medical providers to make unfounded decisions and determinations that could significantly impact the safety and future of their young and vulnerable patients. It emboldens parents to violate their child or teen for the sake of "fact-finding," which can have lasting adverse emotional and mental health effects. And it reinforces the double standard that women and girls must be pure while men and boys can explore and experiment with no regard to self, family, or community. Virginity speculations have caused embarrassment, shame, physical pain, emotional harm, and even death.

Myth 7: Sexual health education increases sexual activity.

A common concern among parents is that education on sexual health might normalize sexual activity and encourage earlier engagement in it. Conservative officials have even implemented policies to restrict or delay period and reproductive health education to certain ages and grades for this very reason. Not only are the age restrictions arbitrarily chosen, but the outcome that these policies purport to prevent is also not real.

Dozens of research studies have evaluated the effects of sexual health education, specifically comprehensive sexuality education (CSE). According to the World Health Organization, CSE is defined as accurate, evidence-based, age-appropriate information about sexuality and sexual and reproductive health. It includes topics like respect, consent, anatomy, puberty, menstruation, contraception, and pregnancy and is deemed critical for health and survival. Research has consistently shown that CSE does not increase or expedite sexual activity in adolescents. In fact, it has been shown to delay initiation of sexual activity and promote safer sexual practices. Benefits include increased condom and contraception use, lower rates of teen pregnancy, lower rates of STIs, and lower rates of sexually active youth. CSE also improves sexual knowledge and attitudes.[6]

The effectiveness of CSE is well established, but even parents who are aware of the benefits may have concerns regarding the best age at which these topics should be introduced. It has been demonstrated that CSE is most effective when provided to younger adolescents, ages fourteen to sixteen, who have not yet initiated sexual activity. For those educated early and often on sexual health and safe practices, delayed initiation of sexual activity and improved contraception use were noted.[7] This evidence suggests that policies should not be pushing to restrict access to sexual education to older children but should instead be working to find the most effective ways to implement reproductive health education earlier in age-appropriate ways.

Finally, sexual education tends to be the only time in which young menstruators are provided information on periods and the management of period bleeding. While period education can certainly be provided without detailed discussions about sexual intercourse, infections, and contraception, it cannot and should not be given without discussion of anatomy, period product use, and pregnancy. Because of the misconception that discussing pregnancy or sex increases risky sexual behavior, critical period education is often affected by these restrictions as well. This can be especially harmful to those children who start puberty around age eight and begin to menstruate as early as age nine. Of note, studies have shown that puberty and menstruation often begin earlier in Black girls. This highlights a racial disparity in delaying reproductive health education, with those starting menstruation at younger ages being the most negatively affected.

Myth 8: Gynecology care is just for adults.

In addition to believing reproductive health education shouldn't be discussed with younger children, many people also believe that gynecological care should be reserved for adults only. And if an adolescent should need to see a gynecologist, the misconception is that it is more than likely related to concerns or effects of being sexually active. This is another by-product of the hypersexualization of women and girls. Period education, health of the female body, and medical care of the gynecological structures and organs are all erroneously reduced to sexual activity.

Many people believe that if a young woman is sick, she must be pregnant. If she has pelvic pain, it must be an STI. If a teen with periods needs to see the doctor, they must be having or preparing to have sex. But the field of gynecology is so much more than that.

There was a time when cardiologists only cared for adults. They cared for adults who primarily had different forms of acquired cardiovascular disease, like heart failure or coronary artery disease. But when improved diagnostic tools allowed for a greater understanding of congenital heart defects, a few cardiologists began to teach themselves how to care for pediatric patients. That's how pediatric cardiology, the first subspecialty board in the field of pediatrics, began in 1938.[8]

Nearly all pediatric subspecialties were created for this reason: to offer necessary specialized care to patients of younger ages. The major difference in pediatric subspecialties and their more adult-focused counterparts is that pediatric patients tend to need care for issues or concerns that they were born with instead of those that developed due to diet, lifestyle, and exposures. The necessity of the subspecialty isn't new; the awareness and focused practice of it is. The same is the case for pediatric and adolescent gynecology.

Gynecology is simply the study and care of the female reproductive health system and its functions. It is worth noting that this is different from obstetrics, which is the care of pregnant people and the management of childbirth. A child does not need to be experiencing pregnancy, sexual activity, or even periods to require gynecological care. Gynecological concerns can and do arise before puberty even begins. Because of how puberty affects the female reproductive organs, major changes occur well before adulthood. The first period, also known as menarche, occurs at an average age of twelve. Because this is the very first period, it requires education on expectations and associated symptoms and guidance for management. This information is critical to preparing children for the next three to four decades of periods they are likely to experience.

Additionally, the onset of periods can uncover a number of health issues. The first period can shed light on everything from endocrine disorders to structural anomalies, chromosomal syndromes, genetic disorders, and even bleeding disorders. The majority of these conditions have significant implications for future health and cannot wait to be addressed until adulthood. Other issues that can't wait for a patient to reach adulthood before receiving treatment include severe period pain, ovarian cysts, vulvar injuries, vaginal irritation and pain, irregular bleeding, PMS, premenstrual dysphoric disorder (PMDD), breast conditions, and more.

The misconception that gynecological care is not appropriate for children and adolescents contributes to delays in diagnosis, inadequate management of pain, prolonged bleeding, prolonged suffering, poor body image, increased risk of diabetes, increased risk of cardiovascular disease, increased anxiety, increased depression, impaired fertility, and even death for young patients. The hesitancy to provide gynecological care to pediatric patients is the result of stigma that is born from sexism, fear, and misinformation. When we understand the legitimate indications and multiple applications of this type of care, we realize pediatric and adolescent gynecology is an incredible opportunity to meaningfully improve the reproductive health and lives of children and young adults.

Isn't that the goal?

Myths about puberty and periods aren't just fun stories or tall tales. They are real beliefs with real consequences. They can be passed down through families and sow deep-rooted fear. They can leave generations of people feeling ashamed, afraid, and alone. They can make what is medically necessary seem socially inappropriate. They can make a comfortable and convenient option seem morally impure. These myths mold minds and inform behaviors. They paralyze some and embolden others. They impact policy, religion, culture, and even health care. Their pervasiveness is why this process of self-reflection is so important.

Before you craft your parenting style, a personal myth subscription inventory must be completed. Any falsehood or misconception you subscribe to should be named, challenged, and unlearned. Only then can we move forward to cultivate an effective and transformative parenting approach. Guidance built on a foundation of misconceptions simply cannot stand. That's why I recommend you build yours on truth, dignity, compassion, kindness, and medical accuracy.

4

Body Basics

A Simple Explanation of Your Child's Anatomy and Why It Is Important for Both of You to Understand It

I was so proud of myself. My expert counseling on contraceptive options had helped yet another undecided postpartum mom choose her new form of birth control before heading home after delivery.

Prior to specializing in pediatric and adolescent gynecology, I completed four years of training in obstetrics and gynecology residency. During this time, I cared for pregnant patients, managed their labors, did their deliveries, and provided their postpartum care. In this case, I'd stepped in to talk with an eighteen-year-old who'd just delivered her first baby two days before. Her pregnancy wasn't planned, and she hadn't had the usual amount of support or visitors that we saw for deliveries. When she gave birth, her aunt stopped by, but only for a few moments. For the rest of her hospital stay, it had been just her and her baby. When we asked her about future fertility plans, she felt strongly that she wasn't ready to be pregnant again anytime soon. But when we asked how she planned to protect herself from pregnancy, she said, "I don't know yet."

Research had shown about half of those that give birth don't make it back for their six-week postpartum appointment. That appointment had historically been the time when we would evaluate their healing, follow up on any medical concerns, and prescribe or insert their preferred form of birth control. Efforts had been shifted to encourage discussion of contraception earlier than the six-week visit, and we had a goal at the hospital where I was in residency to have a plan solidified prior to discharging the patient home. We'd seen many patients who had been very motivated to prevent pregnancy devastated to find out they were already pregnant again by the time we saw them for their postpartum appointment.

It didn't hurt that I genuinely enjoyed contraception counseling and took pride in my ability to explain all the options in a way that centered the patient's personal goals and preferences. I saw contraception as a tool of empowerment and wanted patients to have the information necessary to choose whether and when they would have another child.

After morning rounds, I made my way to this patient's room to see if I could help her make a decision. I did my full spiel, starting with asking how long she wanted to wait before getting pregnant again and how important efficacy was to her. I reviewed her past medical history to look for any contraindications to certain options and talked with her about the risks and benefits of the different types. When I was done, she confidently stated that she wanted to use a hormonal IUD for contraception. I let her know I'd document that preference in her chart and schedule an appointment for her to get the IUD placed. As I was about to leave the room, she said she had one more quick question.

"Ask away," I said, smiling.

"What is the uterus?" she asked.

I cocked my head and squinted my eyes at her, convinced she was joking. But the sincere look on her face confirmed that she was not.

This young girl, now a new mom, had gotten pregnant and carried that pregnancy for over nine months without knowing where the pregnancy truly was. She'd had ultrasounds and even delivered her baby without understanding the organ in which her baby had been growing. I'd strolled my little self-confident behind into her room, presented contraception options, and was about to schedule her for an IUD insertion, all without her knowing where this device was going. She had been failed, by those who raised her, by her community, by her prior doctors, and by me.

I took my hand off the door handle, sat in the chair next to her bed, and spent the next several minutes explaining female anatomy.

In order to effectively navigate or manage any complex system, at minimum, you must understand where things are and how they work. This isn't a foreign concept. It is why manuals for appliances and gadgets all begin with an overview of parts. It is why orientations to new schools or workplaces always include a tour. You cannot effectively care for or participate in something if you don't understand the components that make it what it is. The same goes for our bodies, especially when they're changing.

The biggest hurdle for most parents in orienting their children to their own bodies is knowing where to start. With so many possible emotional, physical, and mental changes, it is easy to get overwhelmed trying to learn them all. The good news is you don't have to. You don't have to know every disorder, medical term, medication, or stage. You don't have to be an expert in anatomy and physiology, but you do need to know the basics. Whether you're a parent who menstruates or not, a foundational knowledge of where things are and how to best care for them is key.

Anatomy is simply the study or understanding of structures. As it relates to reproductive health, it is best to know both the external and internal reproductive structures. Although we encounter external anatomy on a daily basis, with bathing, toileting, and personal care, studies have shown that many people's concrete understanding of external female genitalia is severely lacking. One 2022 study found that only 9 percent of adult female participants could correctly label a diagram of external female genitalia. As troubling as this stat is, it was still greater than the percentage of male participants who could do so.[1]

The understanding of external genital anatomy is often reduced to its sexual utilization and thereby reserved for discussions at later ages. But this delay significantly undervalues the positive impact this knowledge can have on a plethora of other applications, especially when provided early. For example, the most elementary guidance on hygiene is based on anatomy. The long-standing advice to "wipe from front to back" is grounded in the knowledge that we should wipe from the cleaner area to the dirtier one, in this case from the urethra to the anus. By knowing that the anus is more posterior (or toward your back), and the urethra is more anterior (or toward your front), you can infer that wiping back to front could introduce fecal matter from the anus into the urethra or vagina and promote irritation or infection. This fairly natural anatomy-based conclusion is also supported by evidence.

In addition to wiping, anatomy knowledge informs safe grooming practices, appropriate menstrual product use, and proper cleaning techniques. These matters are as age appropriate as their application. If we potty train toddlers, they can and should be taught their correlated anatomy. If periods begin at an average age of twelve and can begin as early as nine, our children and preteens should be prepared with a solid anatomy foundation before their first period. If personal grooming practices begin earlier for gymnasts, swimmers, dancers, or children and adolescents with nonsexual social influences, safe, anatomy-informed grooming guidance should be offered to them too. What is "age appropriate" isn't dictated by age alone. It should be customized to each individual child, family, and situation.

External Anatomy

The external female genital structures are called the vulva. The words *vulva* and *vagina* are often inaccurately used interchangeably.

While the vulva includes the vaginal opening, the vagina itself is considered an internal structure. So yes, the vagina is on the inside. This simple statement has shocked rooms full of adult women. For years, they thought they shaved their vagina, washed their vagina, and even feared exposure of their vagina in shorter skirts and dresses. The mere fact that this is known by so few underscores the non-gender-specific and cross-generational need for the education below. This information isn't just for you to teach your child. It is for you too.

The easiest way to understand the external anatomy is to start with what you encounter first. At the very bottom of the abdomen, just above the rest of the vulvar structures, is the mons pubis. The mons pubis is a tissue mound that is covered in pubic hair and primarily serves as a cushion. At the lower border of the mons pubis, there are two sets of labia or "lips" that are located on either side of the midline. Of note, the midline is the middle of the vulva and is where the three primary openings are located. Other midline human structures include our nose, mouth, and belly button. The larger set of labia are called the labia majora and primarily serve as a protective barrier to the deeper structures. They begin at the mons pubis and end below the vaginal opening and above the anus. During puberty, subcutaneous fat deposition increases to the labia majora, making them plumper, and hair begins to grow along their surface. Both of these changes enhance their protective ability.

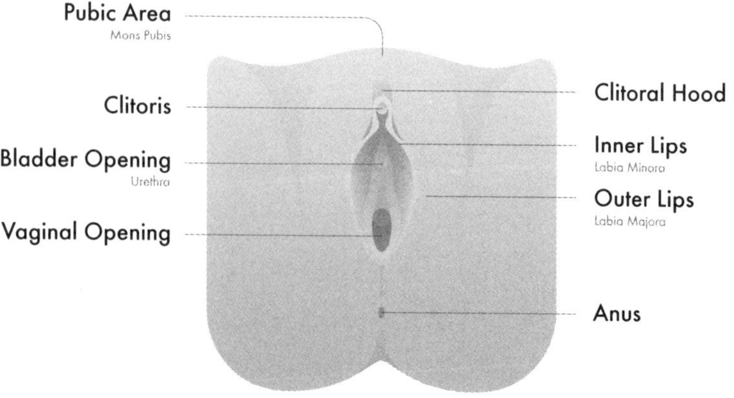

Within the larger labia are smaller labia known as the labia minora. They are thinner and smaller than the labia majora and begin at the clitoris. They lack the hair and fat that the labia majora have and are more delicate and sensitive. The clitoris, which is just above the labia minora, is an important sensory organ. The clitoris has a significant number of nerve endings and is key to sensations of arousal and pleasure. The clitoris is best visualized by gently retracting the skin that overlies it, known as the clitoral hood.

Below the clitoris, located within the labia minora, is the first midline opening, the urethral opening. The urethra is a small tube-like structure that connects to the urinary bladder. It is where urine flows out and is a distinctly different opening than the vagina. This point deserves emphasizing, as it is another poorly understood concept.

When I get my period, will I bleed where I pee from?

Can I pee with a tampon in?

Where do I insert a menstrual cup?

So you're saying there are two different holes?

I have had everyone from preteens to menstruating adolescents and even postpartum adults ask me questions that hinged on the understanding of this anatomical fact—the urethra and vagina are not the same. They are two different structures, one allowing urine to flow out from the bladder and the other allowing menstrual blood to flow from the uterus. Many people are unaware of their separate locations because both openings are located within the labia minora, meaning you would need to spread the labia minora and look closely at your vulva to see them. Just under the clitoris and above the vaginal opening is a smaller, less obvious midline opening. This is the urethra. The urethral opening isn't discussed or identified as much in general anatomy discussions because it doesn't require cleaning or the insertion/removal of products.

The female urethra is significantly shorter in length than the male urethra. Additionally, its close proximity on the vulva to the vagina and anus increases the risk of cross-contamination from vaginal and anal bacteria. The shorter length of the urethra allows for these bacteria to more readily ascend into the bladder and cause infection. For this reason, the risk of bladder infection, also known as urinary tract infection, is higher in females than in males, with a lifetime prevalence of one in three.

Although we may not need to do much with or to the urethra,

its location is still key to understanding things like correct location for menstrual product insertion, UTI risks, and normal anatomy.

Below the urethra is the most important opening for the topic of menstruation and reproduction, the vaginal opening. The vaginal opening can be identified in a number of ways. When spreading the labia, it is the largest and most central opening. When we follow the labia minora downward, they end level to the bottom of the vaginal opening. If we can find the small portion of tissue located between the anus and the vulva, the perineum, the vaginal opening is just above it.

Just inside the labia minora, located at the opening of the vagina, is a thin membranous tissue called the hymen. Despite its small size and absence of biological function, in many cultures, the hymen is a big deal. We touched on this in the last chapter, but the appearance of a hymen is not a reliable predictor of sexual activity. From congenital differences, like hymenal clefts, to nonsexually sustained stretches or tears, the hymen can vary greatly in its shape and size. A normal hymen is one that allows for egress of menstrual blood and insertion of a small tampon. A normal hymen should not completely cover the vagina or require rupturing for use of a menstrual product.

Internal Anatomy

The reproductive structures that we consider to be the internal female anatomy are located within the low abdomen/pelvis. Because we just discussed the external anatomy, we'll start with the vagina. The vagina is an elastic tubular structure that is connected to the uterus via the cervix and extends down to open externally on the vulva. The main purposes of the vagina are for outflow of menses, childbirth, and sexual intercourse. The vagina has a very specific blend of microorganisms and bacteria that help to maintain its naturally acidic pH. Disruption of the vaginal microbiome can lead to abnormal odors, discomfort, irritation, and infection. The vagina is considered to be self-cleaning. Unnecessary exposure to or application of cleansers, fragrances, dyes, and soaps can lead to worsened irritation or infection. For this reason, it is never recommended to clean the inside of the vagina or to douche.

The elasticity of the vagina is primarily due to the presence of estrogen and increases at time of puberty and decreases when estrogen declines in menopause. The average vaginal length is 9 centimeters or 3.5 inches.[2] The top of the vagina is connected to the uterus via the cervix.

The cervix is a shorter, thicker, and firmer structure with a narrow channel that connects the vagina to the uterus. The cervix is a dynamic structure critical to reproductive health and function. Its presence helps to prevent vaginal bacteria from ascending into the uterus, the uterine tubes, or abdomen. During pregnancy, the strength and integrity of the cervix help to keep the developing fetus safely inside the uterus until time for delivery. In labor, the cervix remodels, softens, and dilates to approximately 10 centimeters to allow for vaginal birth. Outside pregnancy, the cervix is essentially closed but can open slightly to allow for passage of menstrual blood during menstruation or entry of sperm during ovulation.

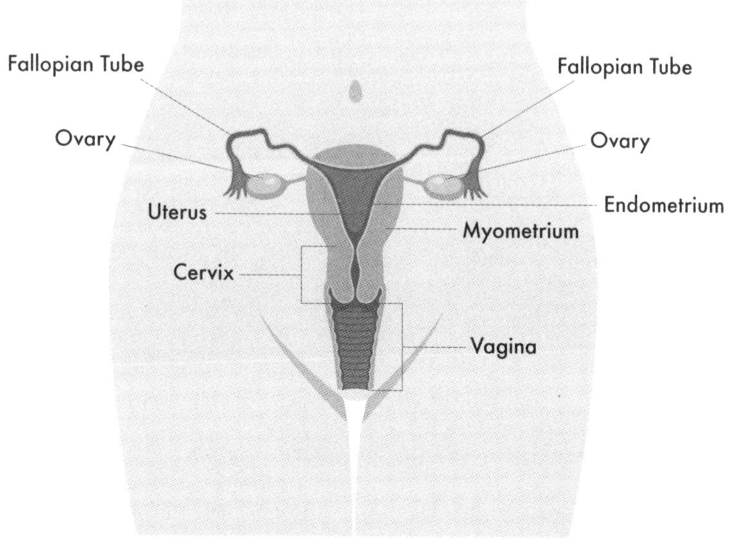

Above the cervix is the uterus. The uterus is a muscle that is shaped a little like a light bulb. The wider portion is the top, or fundus, and it narrows downward toward the cervix. On both sides of the uterus are tubes. The tubes appear almost like pigtails on either side of the uterus, but they are patent tubes with fingerlike projections on the ends. These fingerlike projections are called fimbriae, and they help with the tube's function of picking up the eggs from the ovaries during ovulation. Because of their function, the tubes are usually found draped over the ovaries. They are not, however, attached to the ovaries.

On both sides of the pelvis, attached to both the uterus and the pelvic side wall, are the ovaries. The ovaries are small ovoid structures, and they hold all the eggs. By the time a female infant is born, they have all the eggs that they will ever have. The ovaries do not form new eggs after birth; they house the eggs and begin to release them via ovulation after puberty begins and for the duration of the reproductive years. The ovaries also function by producing and releasing the well-known female reproductive hormones estrogen and progesterone.

Now that we know more about the structures and where they are located, let's discuss how they work together to make menstruation possible.

The Biology of Menstruation

The signaling that triggers the menstrual cycle actually originates in the brain. Because it is a cycle, it has no true beginning or end, but for the sake of discussion, we'll start at the beginning of menstruation. Menstruation is defined as the days of bleeding, which is on average five days in length. The menstrual cycle, however, is approximately twenty-eight days total. It includes the phase where the body grows and matures the next egg (the follicular phase) as well as when the body releases the egg (ovulation) and when the body sheds the uterine lining (menstruation). For this reason, during the reproductive years, one is technically always on their menstrual cycle, even though they are not always menstruating.

The first day of bleeding is considered to be the first day of the menstrual cycle. In fact, when a healthcare professional asks you for the date of your last menstrual period, this is the day that they are looking for. They don't want the last day of your last period or even a range. They want the first day of your most recent period, even if you are currently still on it.

From the first day of bleeding, your body is already working on the next egg. The brain sends the ovary a hormone called follicle-stimulating hormone (FSH) to get the ovary to grow a follicle, or small cyst, around the egg to eventually release it. This hormone from the brain, FSH, helps the ovary to mature the egg. The maturing egg within the ovary promotes the release of estrogen, which works to thicken the uterine lining.

Menstrual Cycle

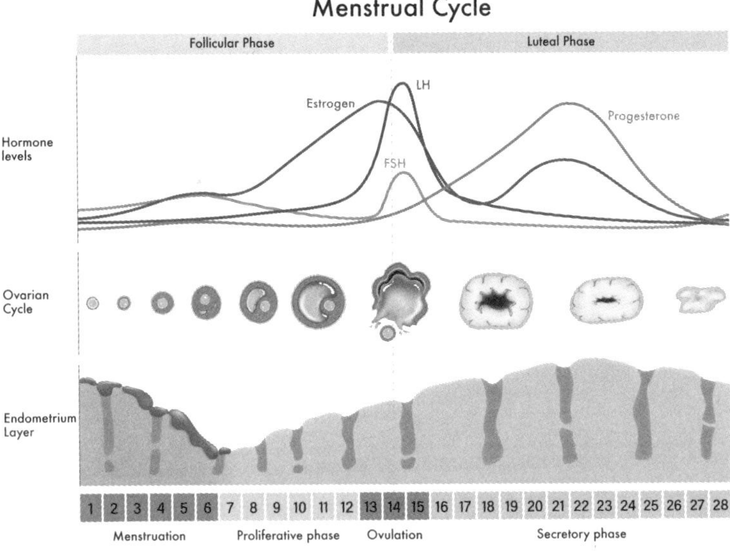

Once the egg is mature enough, the brain sends out a large burst of LH, and the ovary releases the egg via ovulation. Once ovulation occurs, the ovarian follicle that once held the egg begins to release progesterone. During this time, there is a small window (usually about twenty-four hours) when the egg can be fertilized by a sperm. When fertilization doesn't occur, the follicle that was releasing progesterone stops doing so. The sudden decrease in progesterone stimulates the release of inflammatory chemicals that signal for the uterine lining to be shed. The lining sheds in the form of a period, and the cycle repeats.

Menstruation is the body's automatic way of resetting the uterus for the renewed potential for pregnancy. Unfortunately, the uterus has no idea what the goals, preferences, or plans are of the person it resides within. It doesn't care if you are in middle school or in grad school. It doesn't care if you are abstinent or ethically polygamous. It doesn't care if you are in a same-sex partnership or asexual. It doesn't care if you are wearing white pants or on vacation. It is like a subscription that you cannot unsubscribe from. It will come when it is due, when your body's hormones signal for it.

For this reason, while it is not a detox, a signal of womanhood, or a curse, the menstrual cycle is an important marker of general health. If it is expected to be present, it should occur. Unless you are taking hormonal medication that intentionally or knowingly alters the timing of your cycle, it should occur. When it doesn't, investigation is warranted. So paying attention to your period is critical. Managing it safely and effectively is critical to your health as well.

Most menstruators manage their periods with a combination of different products that they've customized over time to fit their flow and lifestyle. Additionally, there is significant variation in period product use based on age, education, socioeconomic status, and geographic location. Since there are dozens of types of menstrual products currently on the market, comprehensive period product discussions can feel overwhelming. Products currently available may be disposable, reusable, inserted, attached, or even incorporated into underwear. Even so, whatever they are and however they are used, they fall into one of two categories—those that absorb and those that don't. We'll discuss this more in the next chapter.

Whether we're discussing period products or anatomy and physiology, a basic grasp of these topics can promote significant clarity and understanding. This chapter alone will help you answer many of the questions your child will have about their changing body. Anatomy helps to answer the questions of where and what, while physiology answers the how and why. By keeping things simple and referencing the provided charts and images, what was once overwhelming and theoretical becomes manageable and concrete. Now we can begin discussing more nuanced topics, where self-awareness is the guiding rule and informed choice is the standard.

5

Everyday Essentials

Understanding Vulvovaginal Health and Period Product Safety

I have a picture. Want to see?" my patient's mom asked, holding up her phone.

"Let's start with just talking, and then I'll look at the picture if I need more details. Is that okay?" I replied.

She nodded in agreement and put her phone back in her bag.

To be clear, I love when my patients use technology to help them share their complaints or covey their history more effectively during appointments. I happily review screenshots of medications, symptom diaries, and period tracking apps, but I learned to exercise a reasonable amount of caution when it came to descriptive pictures. I'm not bothered by most bodily fluids or body parts, but there were a handful of pictures I've been shown that I can never unsee.

"Well, this started a few months ago," she began. "Every time

I do her laundry, there's sticky or dried stuff on the inside of her underwear. I've taught her how to wipe herself appropriately, and I even gave her some feminine wipes to use when she goes to the bathroom, but it is still there. It doesn't stink or anything, but I know it is not normal."

"Okay," I said, nodding to show my comprehension. "And have you noticed this too, Kaley?" I asked, turning my attention to her daughter.

She nodded.

"Does it bother you? Like does it hurt or itch or burn at all?" I asked.

"It doesn't hurt or itch, but it feels weird," she answered.

"Weird how?" I asked her.

"Like wet...like pee," she said, looking a bit embarrassed.

I decided to pivot. "Have you noticed any other changes or new things about your body?" I asked.

She looked over at her mom.

"She's started to wear a training bra and also puts on deodorant every morning," she said, indicating that Kaley had started to have breast development and more body odor as gently as possible so as to not cause further embarrassment.

I nodded to let her know I'd received the hidden message.

"Let me take a look at that picture," I said.

The picture was of a pair of floral cotton underwear with light tan residue in the center. There was no blood, mucus, or any other concerning feature.

I said candidly, "You know, that looks like normal vaginal discharge to me."

Her mom shook her head. "But she hasn't started her period yet."

"No," I said. "But she has started puberty, and she is making her own estrogen. The same estrogen that has caused her breasts to begin forming causes her to start making vaginal discharge."

"So it is not bad hygiene?" her mom asked apologetically.

"Nope. No matter how much she wipes or cleans, she's going to make discharge, and it is going to end up on her underwear. It is normal."

The most important message about hygiene is that we don't need to fix something that is normal. In fact, excessive and obsessive attempts to alter and improve normal bodily processes often lead to the most harm. This is especially true when it comes to vaginal discharge.

Once puberty begins, vaginal discharge is normal and remains normal for the duration of the reproductive years. This means that the mere presence of discharge does not require management or intervention. On the contrary, the presence of discharge signifies a healthy presence of estrogen. When puberty begins, the presence of estrogen triggers several internal and external changes. The most noticeable external change is typically breast development. Internally, however, estrogen causes the uterus to enlarge and the uterine lining to thicken. It also causes changes to the vaginal and cervical cells, promoting increased vaginal wall elasticity and the production of cervical mucus. Vaginal discharge is composed of cells shed from the vaginal lining, water, electrolytes, cervical mucus, and microorganisms. The complex composition of vaginal discharge facilitates its physiological functions to provide vaginal lubrication, protect against pathogens, and maintain overall vaginal health. Thus, vaginal discharge is critical to vaginal health.

Normal vaginal discharge is typically clear or white in color and watery or mucous in consistency. It should not cause vulvar discomfort and shouldn't require the use of a period pad or menstrual product. It may be visible on underwear or even stain it a lighter color, but that's all normal. It is brought on by the presence of estrogen, and estrogen is present well before the first period begins, which means that it is normal for a child or teen to have discharge before they have started to menstruate. This is especially normal and expected if breast development has already begun.

Vaginal discharge changes that we should worry about are increased odor, abnormal color (especially green or yellow), and discharge that causes itching, burning, or discomfort. In these cases, medical evaluation is typically necessary to rule out bacterial or fungal infections. Of note, the diagnosis of a bacterial or fungal infection does not automatically mean a failure in hygiene or personal care. Fungal infections like yeast infections can occur because of other health conditions or after completing a course of antibiotics. Yeast infections are typically associated with thick, chunky white discharge and itching. Bacterial vaginosis is primarily caused by an imbalance in the bacteria of the vagina. This increases the pH of the vagina and causes a characteristic fishy odor along with thin white/gray discharge. Some people with these infections have no symptoms at all.

Vulvovaginal Health

The term "feminine hygiene" greatly annoys me. While there is something legitimate about hygienic practices in that they are intended to promote health and prevent disease, when paired with "feminine," it becomes a phrase that is too often used to shame menstruators into altering what is normal and natural to make it more desirable. This is absurd.

There is no masculine hygiene aisle in the store. Millions of dollars aren't spent on telling men to groom their genitals in a specific way or to clean their groin with a special scented wash. But women and girls are literally preyed on by the feminine hygiene industry. So I'm not going to tell you that you or your child need to smell like fruit or flowers. You don't have to be hairless or perfectly trimmed either. None of these things improve health or prevent infection. In fact, when it comes to matters of vulvar and vaginal health, less is more.

As previously stated, there is no need to clean the internal structure of the vagina. It is self-cleaning in that it has a very specific and complex balance of different microorganisms that all work together to maintain its acidic environment. This resulting acidic state helps to prevent overgrowth of bacteria or fungi, protecting against infection. Products that claim to clean the vagina, balance vaginal pH, or restore bacterial colonization are either presenting false or unsubstantiated claims or causing harm. Douching, for example, has been shown to disrupt the vaginal flora, increase inflammation, and increase susceptibility to infection. It has also been shown to increase the risk of ectopic pregnancy, pelvic inflammatory disease, and bacterial vaginosis, which is associated with an increased risk for STIs and the acquisition of HIV.[1]

Since we know not to clean to vagina, let's discuss what can be cleaned. The vulva, specifically the hair-bearing portion of the mons and the labia majora, warrants cleaning. The skin of this area is not unlike the skin on other parts of your body. Because of the presence of hair and sweat glands, they can hold on to odors, especially in the folds of the groin. To clean this area, you can use just water and a mild soap. Other areas of the vulva that can be cleaned include the area between the larger labia and the smaller labia. Because this area is bordered by the larger fold of the labia majora and the smaller fold of the labia minora, dead skin cells and nonspecific residue can build up here. To clean this area, you can just use warm water and the pads of your fingers to gently remove any buildup. You can also do this under the clitoral hood. Gently retract the clitoral hood, and use warm water and clean fingers to gently remove any residue that may have built up there.

When cleaning the vulva, it is important to avoid getting soap in the area between the labia minora. This area includes the urethral and vaginal openings. Exposure to harsh soaps can cause pain and irritation here. When counseling preteens on cleaning, I tell them to only use soap on the areas that they can wash with their legs still closed. Once you spread your legs apart, the risk of getting soap onto more sensitive surfaces and into more sensitive areas increases.

Additionally, there is no need to purchase a special vulva-specific "feminine" soap. Any mild soap without excessive dyes or fragrances will do. If irritation arises from the use of gentle soaps, warm water only may be best.

Although groin odor has not been shown to directly impact vulvar health, for those with more significant groin odor, an antibacterial soap may work well. Body odor is primarily caused by bacteria. When sweat is released on the skin, bacteria break it down and produce odor from its components. By decreasing the number of odor-producing bacteria on the skin, the intensity of odor is also decreased. It is not generally harmful to use "all-over" deodorant in the groin area, but there is an increased risk of irritation to the groin skin when deodorant is used there. By limiting the use of products with fragrances, dyes, and other harsh chemicals, irritation can be minimized. Beyond the use of deodorant and antibacterial soap, it can be helpful to wear loose underwear as well as breathable fabrics like cotton.

In summary, when it comes to vaginal and vulvar care, less is more. Personal care and cleaning of the vulva should be kept as simple as possible. If using soap for cleaning, avoid unnecessary fragrances, dyes, and harsh chemicals. If using deodorant in the groin area, use as directed, and discontinue use if irritation occurs. When it comes to vaginal discharge, its presence is normal. It is important for there to be a good grasp of normal baseline discharge characteristics in order to be able to recognize when abnormal changes occur. The diagnosis of infections like bacterial vaginosis and yeast infections are not automatically due to poor hygiene and should not be treated as such.

Menstrual Products

In a conceptual sense, period pads have been around since the beginning of time. They've been made of everything from plants to animal skin and old scraps of fabric. Tampons have been around for almost one hundred years. They were introduced to the market in the 1930s and have undergone numerous revisions to improve their safety and effectiveness.[2] Menstrual cups have also been around for decades, providing another safe and effective alternative to traditional absorbent options. With such longevity and familiarity with older options, it is not surprising that some parents are resistant to change.

As a gynecologist caring for the youngest menstruators, I'm always excited for new menstrual products. Whether they help improve comfort or just manage bleeding, I believe the more options we have, the better. My perspective is based on the diverse preferences that I've encountered over the years. I've had patients who would only wear pads, and patients who felt pads were essentially bulky diapers. I have patients who would only wear tampons and patients who wouldn't consider a tampon if it was the last product on earth. I've had patients who would only wear menstrual cups, and I've had patients who felt that cups were medieval torture devices. My respect for patients' personal preferences in how they manage their periods informs my enthusiasm for new and innovative period products. I'm aware enough to know that not everyone feels the same and that not every option will work for every person.

Parents may be resistant to supporting the use of new period products for a number of reasons. One reason is lack of education around how to use, store, clean, or dispose of the product. Newer products like period underwear, for example, are reusable and require washing, drying, and storing like a regular clothing item. Many older menstruators and people over the age of thirty have never even used a reusable period product, let alone chosen a spin cycle setting for one.

Although pads and tampons are still the most commonly used options, a lot of younger menstruators are trying new things. To be clear, there's nothing wrong with using tampons and pads, and we need to understand the safety and appropriate use of them too. But they shouldn't be used just because they're the most established options. The majority of menstruators use a combination of products to manage their periods, and your child should have the opportunity to find what combination of products works best for them. So let's learn more about what they have to choose from.

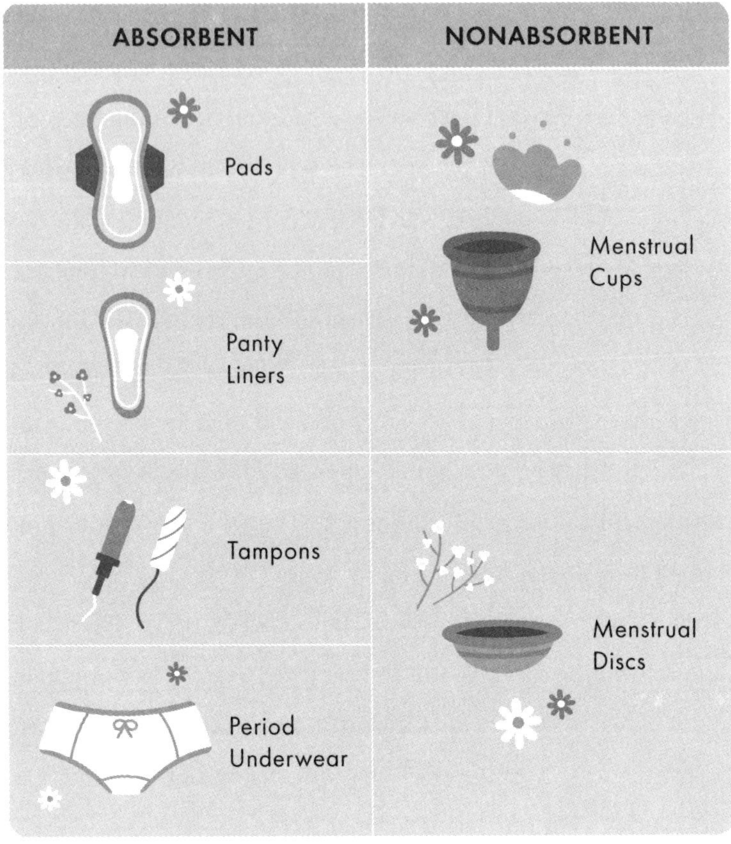

Types of Menstrual Products

Absorbent Menstrual Products

Absorbent menstrual products include pads, panty liners, period underwear, and tampons. These products use different absorbent materials to draw in menstrual blood that would otherwise flow freely onto underwear and clothing. These products are typically made of cotton, rayon, or other synthetic fibers that affect how much and how well they can absorb. They are organized and labeled according to the flow they can accommodate, with lighter flow products being smaller and thinner and heavier flow products being larger and bulkier. Successful use of absorbent products depends strongly on understanding your flow.

Period flow changes throughout the cycle. The first one to two days of bleeding tend to be the heaviest, with the following days slowly lessening in volume. For this reason, it is common for a menstruator to need to use heavier flow items at the beginning of menses and lighter flow products toward the end. Failure to adjust products as period flow changes can lead to discomfort or leaks.

With all externally absorbent period products, basic tenets of hygiene and personal care should be observed. Avoid the use of materials and products that have fragrance, dyes, or harsh chemicals. Use period products only when needed, and discontinue use if irritation or discomfort arise. Change pads every four to six hours, with use of appropriate disposal or storage according to the type of pad used. Wash hands thoroughly before and after use. Lastly, always use the pad or period underwear with the absorbency that correlates to your personal period flow.

Pads

Pads are the most used menstrual product globally. Their popularity is primarily a result of their high acceptability and wide accessibility. Pads tend to be preferred to other period products that require insertion into the vaginal cavity. While this may be due in part to ease of use, it is also a consequence of widespread discomfort with female anatomy and vaginal exploration. In a society where women and girls are expected to observe extremes of modesty and purity, use of an externally absorptive option like a pad doesn't require as much body self-awareness as use of a tampon. And unfortunately, body self-awareness is too often conflated with hypersexuality or immorality.

Pads are also used more commonly because they tend to be the first period product that most menstruators use. Research shows a clear preference for pads for initial menstrual management. Again, this is influenced by ease of use and cultural norms, but it is also by the education and resources available to first-time menstruators. When comprehensive menstrual health education is offered and awareness is increased around other menstrual product options, there is increased adoption of other options.

Although most menstruators use disposable or single-use pads, there are reusable pads that can be temporarily affixed to underwear, washed, and reused. Reusable pads have personal benefits of cost-effectiveness and improved comfort. They are also associated with reduced skin irritation when compared to disposable pads. Reusable pads are used more commonly by people in rural areas, people of lower socioeconomic status, and those with lower levels of education. They are a common intervention in global health initiatives due to their lower cost and longer duration of use. When reusable pads are provided along with comprehensive menstrual health education, stigma is improved, school attendance among menstruators increases, and users report improved satisfaction with their menstrual hygiene.[3]

Panty Liners

Panty liners are essentially smaller, thinner period pads that are reserved for the lightest days of bleeding. Because of their limited absorption, they are primarily used to prevent leaking and staining on underwear. They are a great option for a backup layer when using tampons and a precaution at the beginning or end of menses to capture any unpredictable early or late spotting. Panty liners are not meant to be worn on a daily basis, however. Some people may wear panty liners for management of their normal daily discharge. This is not recommended, because perpetual use can lead to increased vulvar irritation. If you find yourself wanting to wear a panty liner every day due to discharge volume, medical evaluation is warranted to rule out other causes.

Period Underwear

Period underwear combines the sustainability of reusable period pads with the comfort and innovation of intentionally designed underwear. The appeal of period underwear is largely in its comfort, ease of use, and growing accessibility. Period underwear tends to be used by younger menstruators who are environmentally conscious, have higher levels of education, live in urban areas, and have higher socioeconomic status. Although the use of period underwear is cost-effective over time, initial use requires higher up-front costs than other sustainable options. Period underwear also requires more cumbersome maintenance with attention to proper washing and drying techniques to minimize bacterial growth and control odors.

Because you don't have to be on your period to wear period underwear, it is a great option for new menstruators who have more irregular cycles. They can safely wear period underwear around the time that they think they might start their period and worry less about being caught unprepared. Because period underwear can be combined with other products like pads and tampons, those with heavier flows can use period underwear as an extra layer of protection. I especially like period underwear for active menstruators like athletes who don't want to wear tampons but also want to avoid the potential shifting of pads.

Tampons

The final absorbent period product is tampons. Tampons are the second most used menstrual product after pads. They are small cylindrical products made of absorbent material that are inserted into the vagina. They may be inserted with or without the use of an applicator, and they are removed by pulling a small string. They come in various sizes that correlate with their absorbency. Although the sizes noticeably vary in width, tampon sizing is not based on vaginal size. The smallest tampons are for light flow, regular tampons are for light to moderate flow, super tampons are for moderate to heavy flow, super plus tampons are for heavy to heavier flow, and ultra tampons are for the heaviest flows. Even so, new menstruators may find that using the smallest size tampon is helpful when just starting out to learn proper placement and insertion technique.

Tampons are more commonly used by those with higher income and higher education levels. While they tend to be priced higher than pads, they may need to be changed less frequently and could overall be more cost-effective. Of note, there is no such thing as a reusable tampon. All tampons are intended to be used once and disposed of properly.[4]

There are several barriers to tampon use for people with periods. In addition to issues with costs, there are growing health concerns. For decades, human rights organizations have demanded more ingredient transparency from tampon manufacturers. Many major tampon brands list their main ingredients on their websites, but other chemicals present in much smaller amounts are often omitted. Recent studies investigating tampon components revealed trace amounts of metalloids like arsenic and lead as well as dioxins.[5] Of note, these studies failed to show any clinical effects or resulting reproductive health concerns. Multiple medical experts described the concerns around titanium dioxide as exaggerated. The American College of Medical Toxicology published a position statement calling out the limitations of the metalloid study and warning that the mainstream reporting of the study findings contributed to unwarranted concern and worry.[6] Even so, the presence of these potentially harmful chemicals left many menstruators looking for tampon alternatives.

Educational and cultural barriers play a role as well. Many people do not receive adequate menstrual education around the safe and proper use of tampons. Because tampons must be inserted into the vaginal cavity, knowledge of basic female genital anatomy is critical. Most boxes of tampons come with an instructional insert, but that alone may not be enough for someone to feel confident in using them.

A few years ago, after I posted a tampon tutorial video online, I received a private message from a follower thanking me for the information. Although she was a forty-year-old mother of two, she shared that she had never been taught how to use a tampon. She'd always used pads, and as the years went on, she just felt it was too late to learn. But now she had a daughter who had asked to start wearing tampons, and she felt empowered to help her daughter do so because of my video. When we fail to adequately educate menstruators, they sometimes become mothers who were never properly educated. This promotes a cycle of avoidance or fear that continues through generations.

In addition to having a basic understanding of their anatomy, menstruators must also be able to safely and effectively access less accessible parts of their body. For menstruators with limited mobility, cognitive delay, or even visual impairment, tampon use may not be feasible.

As previously mentioned, I used a tampon with my very first period, a fact that some would find horrifying. They'd be even more horrified to know I did this with the encouragement and guidance of my own mom. Due to anatomical misconceptions about the hymen, certain cultures and communities believe that inserting a tampon into the vagina is not possible without rupturing or tearing the hymenal tissue. Once the hymen is torn or broken, they believe virginity is lost, along with social decency, familial pride, and religious purity. They consider tampons to only be appropriate for married women and inappropriate for children, teens, or young adults. Even if there isn't an awareness of all the details, the lore around tampons alone can have parents and guardians forbidding their children from using them.

I ask detailed questions about period history at all my new patient visits. One of those questions is about period products. To ensure I provide the necessary education, I specifically ask if the patient is using tampons. Although I've gotten a variety of responses to this question, when cultural disapproval of tampons is present, the response is always an adamant and fearful denial. When I probe further, I'm typically told something like "not until I'm married" or "my mother doesn't allow it."

While I'm all for parental oversight and respecting household values, I spend a bit of extra time with these families to shed light on the fact that tampons do not and truly cannot take your virginity. I also discuss the evidence-based risks and benefits of tampon use along with guidance for safe and proper use.

Health concerns also exist around tampons and their safety of use. A primary concern for many is the risk of toxic shock syndrome (TSS). TSS is a condition that gained attention in the late 1970s to early 1980s. Around that time, tampon manufacturers were using different synthetic materials to maximize absorbency. These super absorbency tampons were popular because they could be worn for much longer than other tampons on the market. Unfortunately, the material in these tampons created the perfect environment for bacterial overgrowth. The bacteria got into the bloodstream of the tampon wearer, released a deadly toxin, and caused severe systemic damage. Symptoms included a high fever, rash, nausea, vomiting, and muscle aches. By 1982, 1,660 cases of TSS had been identified, and 88 had resulted in death. Of the total cases, 96 percent involved women, and 92 percent began during menstruation. The average age of female patients affected was twenty-three, and the overwhelming majority of patients were white.[7]

Once the connection was made between TSS and tampons, the super absorbency tampon involved was removed from the market, and tampons, along with their instructions for use, changed forever. The tampons of today do not include the bacterial growth–promoting materials that they included in the '70s and '80s. Tampons now have much lower absorbency and have very clear absorbency labeling. The Centers for Disease Control and Prevention also issued recommendations to reduce TSS risk. These include washing hands prior to insertion, changing each tampon every four to eight hours, never exceeding eight hours of wear, using the lowest absorbency level necessary to manage your period blood flow, and wearing tampons only when on your period.[8] Studies have also shown that menstruators who alternate between tampons and pads have lower risk of TSS when compared to those who wear tampons exclusively. This new knowledge and associated interventions have helped to lower the risk of TSS with tampon use to less than 1 in 100,000. But there's an important point that needs to be clarified in this narrative.

Tampons do not actually cause TSS. TSS is caused by the bacterium *Staphylococcus aureus* (staph), specifically the strain that produces the TSS toxin or TSST-1. One in every five people, or 20 percent of the population, is colonized with staph, meaning they have it in or on their body without associated symptoms or illness. Staph is a very common pathogenic bacterium and is the most common cause of food poisoning. It is naturally found in a variety of places on the human body, including on the skin, in the nose, in the gastrointestinal tract, and on the perineum.[9]

Nonmenstruating females and males have been diagnosed with TSS. TSS can be seen in those with postsurgical infections, indwelling catheters, pacemakers, and other minor traumas. In fact, most cases today are not associated with tampons or menstruation at all.

Even so, the correlation between TSS and tampons has led to a long-standing fear of tampon use that crosses generations. Without fully understanding what TSS is, people have sworn off using tampons in the name of safety and caution. They also share the same guidance with their children, not fully grasping how much has changed in the past fifty years.

As a gynecologist who cares for our youngest menstruators, I explain to both parents and patients that tampon use, when done properly, is perfectly safe. Instructions for the safe use of tampons are slightly more involved than the use of pads because the stakes are higher. When it comes to tampons, I give my patients the following advice:

TAMPON TIPS
Only use tampons if you are comfortable with your anatomy and can access the vaginal opening without difficulty.
Only use tampons when you are on your period.
Change your tampon every four to six hours. Never exceed eight hours of wear.
Always use the lowest absorbency level necessary. If you can wear a tampon without changing it for a full eight hours, you should step down to a smaller size.
Never go to bed wearing a tampon. Teenagers can notoriously sleep well beyond eight hours. Falling asleep overnight while wearing a tampon increases the risk of prolonged wear.
Wash hands before and after inserting a tampon.
Alternate between tampons and pads if possible.

Tampons offer a number of benefits to menstruators who wear them, including improved comfort, better leak protection, use while swimming or doing water sports, and discreet wear in more formfitting uniforms, costumes, or clothing. Yes, avoidance of tampons altogether will definitely prevent tampon-related TSS, much like never flying in planes will prevent injury or death from a plane crash. Parenting is about raising children to think critically and make decisions that promote their safety, align with their values, and lead them toward their future goals. This requires nuance, collaboration, and understanding. If your child wants to try out tampons, an overwhelmingly negative response may cause them to avoid future discussions on period products or personal care. The medical opinion is that tampons are safe. You and your child must decide what works best for your unique needs.

Nonabsorbent Menstrual Products

Two remaining period products make up the nonabsorbing group. These are menstrual cups and menstrual discs. Menstrual discs and cups are simple products in that they just hold or store menstrual blood. They do have to be inserted into the vaginal cavity, however, and that requirement tends to be the major barrier to their use. Menstrual cups and discs are used much less commonly than pads and tampons. In addition to their more complex insertion process, many people don't use these products due to lack of education and awareness.

Menstrual Cups

Menstrual cups have been around for several decades, although their increased use occurred around the early 2000s. A menstrual cup is a small bell-shaped cup typically made of medical-grade silicone that is inserted into the vagina in a way that allows the rim of the cup to sit flush against the walls of the vagina to collect blood and prevent leakage. They are great for those with heavier flows who would prefer to change their product less often. They are also ideal for those seeking a more environmentally sustainable option or just wanting to use something different from pads, tampons, and liners.

Because of the necessary rigidity of menstrual cups, although they are flexible, they must be bent or folded in order to be inserted and removed. The nature of their insertion may be challenging for someone who has difficulty with their hands or limited hand strength. They may also be challenging for someone with long nails or extravagant nail art. Menstrual cup removal has been associated with inadvertent removal of IUDs, so caution should be used for those with IUDs in place. The best part about menstrual cups is that they can be worn for up to twelve hours and can be rinsed or wiped clean and reused. After your period ends, the cups can be sterilized by boiling and stored for later use. Depending on the brand and type, one menstrual cup can last up to ten years.

Menstrual Discs

Menstrual discs have a flatter, more concave shape. Some menstrual discs are single use, while others are reusable. Discs can be pinched to be inserted more easily than menstrual cups but must be tilted up and tucked behind the pubic bone to remain in place.

If not placed properly, leaking can occur. Because of their greater flexibility and location of placement, some menstrual discs boast an auto-emptying feature. They suggest that the disc can tip forward to partially empty if the wearer simply bears down (like when pushing out a bowel movement). This can help avoid the need to manually remove the disc along with the potential mess.

Menstrual discs can be worn for up to twelve hours and hold more blood than most pads or tampons. One popular disc boasts that it can hold as much as five super tampons. This means a menstruator can work a full twelve-hour shift, fly on an eleven-hour transcontinental flight, or sleep a full ten-hour night without having to change their disc. This also means that three discs could essentially replace a full box of tampons when it comes to flow capacity. This is a huge deal for menstruators with heavy bleeding.

The biggest downside to menstrual cups and discs can be their removal and the process of discarding menstrual blood. Since these products do not absorb the blood, the risk of spills is higher than with absorbing products, and use in public restrooms without private sinks can be tedious. Even so, they are the most sustainable and cost-effective options of all menstrual products, with a menstruator potentially using the same product for several years. Many studies show that menstrual cup use increases when education about them and access to them is provided. This evidence supports the idea that menstrual cups would be used by more people if they had greater awareness of their use and benefits.

The ultimate goal of menstrual product education is to provide parents and their children with all the options necessary to choose the best products for them. Many adults end up preferring a different menstrual product than they did when they were younger. Many people use multiple types of products during one menstrual cycle, adjusting for flow, comfort, planned activities, and more. What works for one person may not work for another. There is no need and honestly no room for unfounded judgment in the menstrual product space. Use what makes you feel comfortable, safe, and protected. Use the product that supports your beliefs around sustainability and environmental consciousness. Use the product that fits your flow and your lifestyle. Every menstruator, regardless of how old they are, where they live, or how much money they have, deserves to menstruate with dignity.

6

Prepare for Puberty

What to Expect to Happen When So You're Not Caught by Surprise

"Just a heads-up, emotions are pretty high in there."

I looked up at my nurse for more details.

"The patient is fine. It is the mom who keeps crying," she added.

I frowned as I looked down at the intake form. The reason for the visit simply read "first period."

"Hi," a bright-eyed girl exclaimed as I walked in. She wiggled in her seat with childlike energy, causing the beads at the ends of her hair to rattle.

"Hi there!" I responded.

I noticed her mother was still dabbing at the corners of her eyes when I sat down. When her eyes met mine, she managed to force a brief smile before bursting into tears again.

"Tell me what's on your mind," I said gently while handing her more tissues.

"I didn't know it would be this hard," she began. "It feels like she was just in diapers, and now she's a woman!" She sobbed. "I wasn't ready when it happened to me, and I'm not ready now that it is happening to her."

The girl wrapped her arms around her mother and looked at me. It pained me to detect a mixture of remorse and confusion on her face. She looked remorseful for having caused her mother distress but also confused about what she'd done wrong.

The girl's name was Trinity, and she was eleven years old. Her listed hobbies included doing TikTok dances and making bracelets. She'd had two periods so far, and they began about eighteen months after she started wearing her first training bra. Although she was already at adult height, her innocence and merriment were almost contagious.

This was no woman. This was a child.

I learned that Trinity's mom had experienced her first period before she felt prepared and had done so in an environment where menstruation signified womanhood. For her, the onset of periods was a negative event that brought on involuntary physical and relational changes. Due to this experience, she felt powerless and afraid. This caused her to resent her own period and avoid the opportunity to prepare her daughter for menstruation, leading to the belief that her daughter's first period would signal the loss of her baby. So when Trinity began to menstruate, her mom grieved the event, centering her own perceived loss instead of offering compassion and guidance to her daughter when she needed it most.

I asked Trinity to step out of the room and wait with my nurse while I spoke with her mother alone. I started by acknowledging her feelings and reassuring her of an important fact. Not only was Trinity still her baby, she also needed her now more than ever before. I also provided a clear warning that because of her mother's emotional response, Trinity was beginning to have a negative period experience. If she thought her period caused her mother pain and sorrow, she would learn to resent her period. She might also view herself as abnormal, even though her puberty cadence was perfectly normal. Trinity had not started her period too soon. Her mother just didn't know the signs to recognize when it was coming.

"I thought we had more time" is one of the most common statements that parents make when they find themselves unprepared for their child's first period. While I find this to be a sincere defense, my heart still breaks as I imagine the fear and confusion their child must have felt when they started bleeding without explanation. And when this occurs, the parent usually must scramble to provide period products, clothing changes, and physical comfort items. Amid the heightened chaos and emotions, they often postpone the necessary menstrual education in favor of crisis management. Everything from that point on is reactive instead of proactive, intervention instead of prevention. To the relief of both the parent and child, the first period eventually ends. They settle into the comfort of their normal routine, and the education is often never revisited.

One of the greatest frustrations in my line of work is the

perpetual denial of physical and emotional changes that are expected and inevitable. I will never fully understand the shock and surprise that many parents feel when their growing child eventually grows right into having periods. From the very first day that you learn you are carrying a female fetus or adopting a daughter or you have birthed a baby girl, you should know that puberty and therefore periods are coming. Much like the infant milestones of social smiling, rolling over, and sitting up, puberty is a milestone that is expected to occur as a part of normal, healthy development. In fact, you'd most likely be extremely alarmed if your child never went through puberty. You would be frantically searching for answers online and seeking out prompt medical evaluation.

So what's the issue?

I believe lack of parental preparation is due to one of three reasons: grief around the idea of losing their "baby," uncertainty about when to expect puberty to occur, and discomfort about how to start the conversation with their child.

After giving birth to my own child, I better understand how jarring it can be to imagine the sweet, cuddly baby in your arms as a pubertal adolescent. I fully resonate with the sentiments that *time moves too quickly* and *the days are long, but the years are short*. With every increase in onesie size, I feel the tiny newborn I brought home from the hospital fading further and further away. And while this might trigger emotions of longing or sadness, it does not prevent me from taking care of my child's present needs. My emotions may lag, but my parenting and provision of daily needs cannot. Regardless of how it makes me feel, my child needs me as a constant protector, comforter, and guide.

Constant needs can be challenging to meet in the face of change. And pubertal change, admittedly, can be hard to anticipate. While you may not be able to nail down exactly when your child's puberty will begin, a decent predictor is maternal age of menarche or first period. Studies have shown that earlier age of maternal first period is predictive of earlier pubertal onset in that woman's female children.[1] So if the maternal parent has a history of menarche at age eleven, it may be reasonable to expect puberty to begin around age nine. Even if you can't predict exactly when puberty will start, you can predict how it will progress and when periods should begin.

The timing, pattern, and cadence of female puberty have been extensively studied for many decades. Although it is well established, it is important to note that timing can vary by race, ethnicity, and environmental factors. For example, the average age of pubertal onset in the United States is ten years in white females and nine years in Black females. Additionally, higher body mass index is associated with earlier pubertal onset. In recent years, pubertal onset has trended toward younger ages. This is believed to be due to increased exposure to endocrine-disrupting chemicals as well as the long-standing issue of increasing rates of childhood obesity.[2] Understanding how these factors influence pubertal onset may help you estimate when your child will begin to experience pubertal changes. Moreover, adequate awareness of your child's current pubertal stage can help you predict and plan for what's to come.

The Three Stages of Female Puberty

THELARCHE
Breast development

MENARCHE
Onset of periods

PUBARCHE
Pubic hair growth

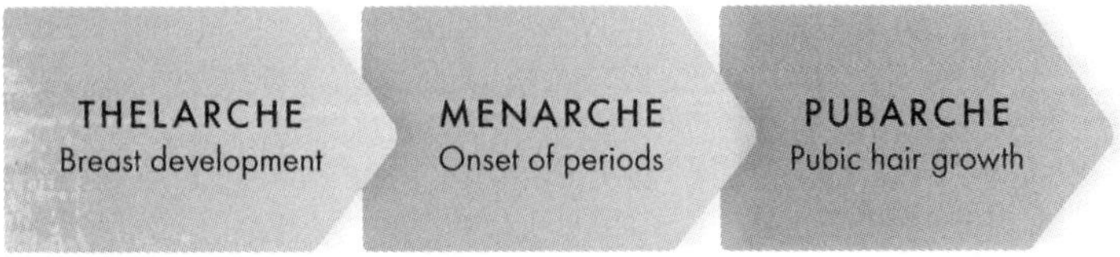

Stage 1: Breast Development

There are three main stages of female puberty: breast development (thelarche), pubic hair development (pubarche), and the start of periods (menarche). A prepubertal female child has no breast development and no pubic hair. This is expected for biological females ages zero to seven years. Puberty typically begins between the ages of eight and thirteen. The typical pattern of female puberty begins with breast development. Thelarche typically begins at an average age of about ten years old.

To better understand breast development, we must discuss Tanner staging. Dr. James Tanner was a child development specialist who extensively studied female physical pubertal changes during the 1940s. He created a sexual maturity rating system that still serves as an objective way to classify and track pubertal progression. The scale is from 1 to 5, with 1 being the prepubertal form and 5 being the adult form.

Tanner stage 1 of breast development is no development at all. There's no palpable breast tissue, and the nipple and areola have no change in shape or color. Stage 2 is characterized by the development of a breast bud under the areola. The breast bud is a small, palpable growth of breast tissue that can occur symmetrically and can be tender to the touch. This is the first sign of puberty in female children. Stage 3 of breast development is characterized by growth of the breast mound. This is when breast tissue starts to grow outside the areola, creating more of a mound appearance, but still with no change to the areola or nipple. Stage 4 of breast development is where the breast mound has formed, but the areola and nipple form a second smaller breast mound on top of it. Stage 5 is when the nipple protrudes beyond the areola, and the areola is now smooth and level with the rest of the breast mound but darker in color.

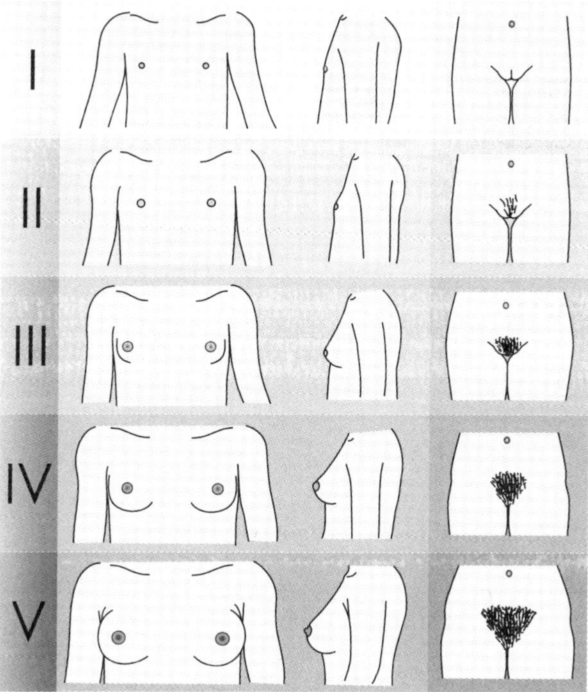

Tanner stage 2 is where it may become more comfortable for girls to wear an undershirt or training bra. This is mostly because breast buds can be tender, and it may be uncomfortable when a shirt or top rubs across them. Additionally, breast buds can be visible through thinner material. Although there is nothing inherently wrong with visible budding through clothing, your child may feel self-conscious or even embarrassed by their changing body and prefer the concealing quality of an extra layer.

A general rule of thumb is that periods typically begin about two years after breast development begins. This is not a rigid standard and should not be applied as such. Periods can begin as soon as one year or as late as three years after breast development begins. The point is to recognize that once breast development starts, periods are well on their way.

This makes sense, because breast development is a sign of estrogen presence. Estrogen must first be present to increase the size of the uterus and even thicken the uterine lining before the first period can ever occur. Because of the important effects of hormones, it is necessary and natural for periods to begin after breast development has started. The first period of menarche usually occurs during Tanner stage 4.

Stage 2: Pubic Hair Development

The second stage of puberty is pubarche, or the development of pubic hair. This typically begins about one to one and a half years after thelarche. Similar to the staging of breast development, Tanner stage 1 pubic hair development is no pubic hair at all. Tanner stage 2 is where pubertal change begins with growth of sparse hair, mostly on the labia majora. Tanner stage 3 is where the hair becomes darker, curlier, and coarser, covering more of the labia majora and extending upward toward the mons pubis. Tanner stage 4 is fuller growth of hair in an inverted triangle but not extending to the thighs. Tanner stage 5 is adult form with full growth of pubic hair that extends to the inner thighs. Menarche usually occurs once pubic hair has progressed to Tanner stage 3 or 4.[3]

Stage 3: Menstruation

The third stage of puberty is menarche, or the first period. The first period experience can differ from person to person. We know some people have cramps prior to starting their first period, and others report not having or not noticing any cramping. The color of the blood can also differ. It is not uncommon for first period blood to be brown or even black in color. Additionally, this first episode of bleeding may last for only two to three days. Because it might not resemble the typical bright red bleeding that lasts five to seven days, some people may not immediately realize they have started menstruating. It's estimated that 98 percent of females have experienced menarche by age fifteen. For this reason, the absence of periods by age fifteen warrants medical evaluation.[4]

Periods can often be a bit unpredictable for the first one to three years after menarche. This is because regulation of menses is dictated by appropriate signaling and communication between the hypothalamus, pituitary, and ovaries. This is referred to as the HPO axis. When periods first start, the HPO axis is not well established and doesn't function consistently. This is referred to as being "immature." An immature HPO axis causes some cycles to occur without ovulation, or release of the egg. These early anovulatory cycles can be unpredictable in frequency and duration. In fact, they can cause periods to skip months or cause bleeding that lasts for weeks. This usually resolves without intervention, and maturity of the HPO axis eventually leads to regulation of cycles. Even so, the old saying that "anything goes" in the first couple of years of menstruation is not true. Prolonged bleeding can be especially dangerous and can have very serious adverse health effects. For this reason, even expected cycle irregularities shouldn't be ignored.

Because each stage has distinct characteristics, with a little observation, you should be able to determine where your child is in their pubertal progression. By doing so, you will then be able to estimate how long you may have until periods begin. In the meantime, age-appropriate and stage-appropriate discussions can and should begin.

How to Start the Conversation Early

Children start to notice physical differences in boys and girls when they are as young as two to three years of age. They can use these observed differences to typically identify themselves as belonging or not belonging to a certain gender by the age of three.[5] Additionally, toilet training or potty training typically begins around this age, with awareness and discussion around genitalia. For this reason, introduction to basic anatomy can be age appropriate even for toddlers. Many child development specialists advocate for teaching children the appropriate terms for genitalia from the outset. Using the correct language for each body part helps to increase awareness that these areas are different from other areas like the knee, forehead, or ankle, for example. Because they are different, they require different care and have different rules. This is especially important for learning protective concepts like appropriate and inappropriate touch. While most parents don't want to think about anyone ever trying to harm or abuse their child, this type of guidance helps a child to recognize abnormal behavior, describe that behavior accurately, and report the interaction promptly if it were ever to occur.

The concept of "private" and "don't touch" areas is continued on through the remainder of the prepubertal years and reinforced with things like bathroom stalls, dressing rooms, and even swimwear. We wait to remove our clothes until we enter the bathroom stall to keep private areas private when using the toilet. We try on clothing or change our outfits in dressing rooms because they offer privacy, which makes us feel comfortable and safe. For biological females, our swimsuits cover our private areas, bottoms, and chests, while our friend's or sibling's might just cover their private area and bottom. This is because chests that will grow breasts are private too. Although one could argue that the prepubertal female chest doesn't need to be covered, societal norms often dictate otherwise.

The best time to start discussing physical pubertal changes is when your child or their peers start experiencing them. While they may very likely bring these topics or observations up to you, an easy conversation starter can simply begin with "Have you noticed…"

"Have you noticed any changes in your classmates this year?"

"Have you noticed any of your teammates wearing bras or undershirts under their uniform?"

"Have you noticed hair growing in new places on you or any of your friends?"

You can also ask more pointed questions like "Have any of your friends started to shave their underarms or legs?" or "What do you know about deodorant?" or "How have you been feeling about your body?"

Children are more observant than we often give them credit for, and they've likely noticed and developed a general thought or opinion around what they've seen. By asking questions, especially open-ended questions that promote a response beyond a yes or no, you can gauge their understanding of these topics before launching into education. This is also a great time to correct any myths or misconceptions that may be taking root.

Unsurprisingly, the conversations between preteens on matters of sexual and reproductive health are riddled with inaccuracies and falsehoods. The addition of social media and online exposure only worsens this fact. Creating a safe space where your child feels they won't be judged by what they share or what they ask will usually produce the best opportunity to fact-check, redirect, and reassure them.

This is a great time to introduce the increased personal care and hygiene measures that puberty has made or will make necessary. Because perspiration and body odor increase in puberty, deodorant needs to be added to your child's daily routine, along with an extra shower after exercise or outdoor play. Because the skin on their face is producing more oils and acne, a skin-care regimen including a face wash and moisturizer will likely need to be added in the morning and at night. After the development of breast tissue, a training bra or undershirt may need to be worn under their usual clothing. New hair under their arms or on their legs may lead to a desire for hair removal. Discussing safe options for hair removal and why, how, and if removal is needed can occur now as well.

Other discussions around puberty management may occur according to unique needs and curiosities. Remember, curiosity isn't a crime. If it is happening to the people around them, it is natural for your child to be curious about it, which means it is definitely time for you to address it.

As we discussed, periods are one to two years away once breast development begins. This is the time to start discussing what periods are, what happens when they start, and how to manage periods and their associated symptoms. If you have already discussed female genitalia, private areas, and pubertal changes like hair growth, training bras, and body odor, this conversation is not the first of its kind. You have an established framework for safe discussions on body changes that have helped to build trust and understanding. This foundation for communication has been based on preparedness, safety, confidence, health, and happiness. This helps to ensure period discussions honor these same aspects without undue emphasis on sex, negative behaviors, infections, or pregnancy.

Early preparation for menarche has well-established benefits. When adolescents are provided comprehensive menstrual education and access to period products, they have increased knowledge, better hygiene, and better school attendance. Increased knowledge means they understand what the vulva is and where the vagina is. It means that they know how to insert a tampon or menstrual cup, and they know how long to wear it and when to change it. Better hygiene means they wash their hands before and after using a menstrual product. They know how and where to discard their used products and how to clean and safely reuse their reusable ones. Better school attendance means a better chance at high scholastic achievements. It means they don't have to play catch-up with their school lessons or miss a big test, presentation, or project because of their period.

Education that encourages open dialogue on menstrual health and sharing of concerns is shown to increase willingness to discuss menstrual topics as well as recognition of what is normal.[6] This means more adolescents have tough conversations about what it feels like to go through these physical changes. They hold space for peers who have heavier bleeding, suffer from gender dysphoria, or endure significant period pain. They have a clear understanding that it is normal to experience some breast tenderness, bleeding that varies in color and consistency, and cyclical changes in acne, mood, and vaginal discharge. They ask for help when pain is unbearable, bleeding is irregular, and mental health is impaired.

When menstrual health is normalized, attitudes shift, and stigma decreases. It has specifically been demonstrated that period education helps to challenge negative and limiting beliefs around what one is capable of doing on their period.[7] This means your child may decide to run for student government representative even though they will be on their period when they give their big speech. This means they can show up and make the All-American team at cheer camp even though they're experiencing PMS. This means they may stop hiding their tampon in their sleeve when they have to go to the restroom and walk boldly down the halls instead, knowing that they're doing what needs to be done to manage a totally natural process.

When education is offered to kids, anxiety, fear, and embarrassment around menstruation decrease.[8] This means they can regulate their breathing and relax their shoulders even though their period tracker has notified them that their period should be coming soon. This means a period stain or leak doesn't trigger overwhelming panic or thoughts of self-harm. It also means that they aren't afraid to tell a parent or trusted adult that their period makes them nauseous, unable to stand, or dizzy.

Menstruators have been noted to have improved comfort and increased confidence and agency when they receive menstrual health education.[9] This means they don't feel the need to dissociate from their changing body. Instead, they embrace it. They feel ownership over their body and make choices that will promote their physical health and safety instead of compromise it. They may also be more likely to leave situations and relationships where they aren't valued and treated properly. All these benefits are noted when menstruation is acknowledged, explained, and normalized.

While the majority of the studies that demonstrate the benefits of menstrual health education are conducted in a research setting, the positive impact of this kind of education isn't limited to only school programs, community organizations, and healthcare settings as sources. Parental involvement and support in period education yields similar results. Menstruators who received guidance from their parents were less likely to have anxiety and embarrassment about menstruation. Young menstruators who discussed menstrual hygiene with their parents had better menstrual hygiene practices and knowledge.[10] And with the current political acts of banning books on reproductive health and limiting menstrual education in school, the role of parental involvement is becoming increasingly important.

The school program where your oldest daughter learned basic health concepts may not exist for much longer. The book in the school library that detailed helpful anatomy may no longer be allowed on the shelves. The community program that hosted an annual period party may no longer be eligible for necessary funding. Reproductive health as we know it has gotten caught in the crosshairs of politics, and our youngest and most vulnerable menstruators are suffering as a result.

But thank God for parents.

You know your child better than anyone else does. You know

their strengths, weaknesses, motivations, and fears. You also know your family and faith values. You know how you want your child to be raised, the principles that should be foundational to their daily life, and how much you love and respect them as individuals and as human beings. You set the standard for how they should be treated by others and for how they should treat themselves. You are their first teacher of self-respect, self-discipline, and unconditional love. You are their safe space, their safety net, and their emergency contact. You are the constant in a polarizing and bickering world. You are their home base and who they look to for centering. Your role has never been more important than it is right now.

This is why this book is written for you. Because your knowledge, confidence, and comfort around reproductive health directly impact that of your child. Well-informed parents who are comfortable discussing menstrual health are more likely to support their children, have open conversations, and provide accurate information. Educating parents on menstruation reduces parental anxiety and improves positive attitudes, aiding in effective communication between parents and their menstruating adolescents. Parents who communicate more effectively promote better menstrual health practices.

Conversely, increased parental anxiety leads to increased adolescent anxiety. Parents who are anxious about menstruation create environments of fear and discomfort around the topic.[11] This fear and discomfort lead to increased stress and worsened depression and anxiety. Early menstrual health education and parental guidance help mitigate these issues, with improved mental health, decreased stress, and improved confidence.

Despite a strong desire to know more about menstruation, 30–40 percent of menstruators will have their first period without getting adequate education beforehand.[12] This means they will start bleeding and not know why it is happening or what to do about it. This is unacceptable. It is well established that earlier menstrual education is more effective than education that is provided after the first period begins. It is human nature to want to be given information about a significant change before it happens. Knowledge decreases fear, improves confidence, and allows for preparation. When you are prepared, you feel a sense of power, pride, and control.

As I said, your role as parents and guardians matters more than ever during these pivotal years. Your role isn't supplemental; it is foundational. Your knowledge isn't complementary; it is critical. Your influence isn't optional; it is vital.

7

How to Show Up in All the Right Ways

Supporting Your Child Unconditionally During Puberty and Their First Period

I speak with people often about their first period experience, and I have yet to meet one who couldn't recall at least some detail about it. When they do, it is not so much about how much they bled or whether they experienced any physical pain; it is typically about how they were made to feel.

During a church health fair, a woman in her fifties shared with me that her mother responded to her first period with intense anger and accused her of causing her periods to start early because she was thinking too much about boys. This made her feel profound guilt, and she carried the shame with her for years.

A young woman on Instagram remembered that she got her first period while her mom was at work. When she told her dad, he instructed her to lie down with her legs up in the air until her mom got home. This made her feel helpless and confused and did nothing to manage the bleeding.

A former patient of mine recalled that her mom sobbed for days when she started her first period. She felt so bad for upsetting her that she decided not to ask her mom any of the several questions she had. She spent months avoiding the topic, fearing the sorrow it might cause and bearing the distress all on her own.

A colleague shared that her mom "lost it" when she got her first period. She didn't go into detail, but she added that their relationship was never the same. The pain in her eyes revealed a deep emotional wound, one that was unhealed and forever tied to a natural and entirely involuntary event.

While the experience of a first period and its associated effects are very real, each of these stories is the subjective account of one person. Moreover, memories like these tend to be inherently imperfect, subconsciously amended, and impossible to corroborate. For this reason, I make an effort to assume the best of the parents involved. I assume that these parents didn't harbor ill will toward their children or craft their responses maliciously. I assume the father of the woman on Instagram had no clue what to do and truly felt that challenging gravity was the best approach to managing his child's first period. I assume my patient's mom didn't want to be upset about her daughter's maturation but truly could not stop crying. I also am willing to bet not one of them ever realized the extent of the harm they caused.

Parents may find themselves in a panic when their child gets their first period for a number of reasons. Stigma and shame, for example, can play a huge role in a parent's hesitation to discuss menstruation. If they've always considered the menstrual process to be taboo, they may feel panic when addressing it becomes unavoidable. Fathers and nonmenstruating parents have traditionally been excluded from menstruation conversations. As a result, they may experience greater difficulty in communicating with their children about it than mothers or menstruating parents do. This reluctance may be due to lack of menstrual education and experience and may lead to overwhelming fear that they just don't know enough to be helpful. Another reason parents may panic is because they're afraid that their child will panic. They may fear that their child will be confused, afraid, or even ashamed by their period. The perceived lack of control over their child's response can be too much for a parent to bear.

But there's good news. You have prepared for this. This is not an unpredictable or unexpected event. Hopefully, you've been speaking openly and honestly with your child about their body and their pubertal changes for a while now. You've learned the basic anatomy, the different stages of puberty, the process of the menstrual cycle, and the different menstrual products. More importantly, you've established safe and open communication with your child, so they know to come to you when their first period arrives. They won't be confused about what's happening, and they won't be afraid because they know you'll be right there supporting and guiding them.

I'm telling you not to panic because there's truly no need to.

I'm also telling you not to panic because your response to their first period will have a lasting impact on them.

Negative parental response to menarche isn't an isolated phenomenon. It is a global issue that has been shown to significantly impact adolescent mental health across a variety of cultures. A study of Mexican American fifth graders ages nine to eleven showed that harsh parenting exacerbated symptoms of anxiety and depression. It also worsened conduct problems and oppositional defiance. Harsh parenting was determined by reports from both the child and the parent, with each providing a rating for frequency of behaviors like screaming at the child when they did something wrong. The negative impact of harshness was especially pronounced in those who were early maturing. This meant high levels of maternal harshness actually amplified the negative effects of earlier pubertal timing.[1]

Harsh parenting isn't unique to Mexican culture and has been frequently reported by those who had upbringings in immigrant households of many cultures and ethnicities. Some of the leading narratives about first-generation parenting on social media center around a common toughness or coldness resulting from the extremely difficult conditions that these parents had to face in order to enter a new country and build a new life. In these communities, a hardened personality isn't considered to be as much of a shortcoming as it is a necessity for survival. Even so, subsequent generations feel the negative effects of this type of parenting.

In the United States, adolescents of Mexican descent often experience puberty earlier than their non-Hispanic white counterparts.

Earlier pubertal timing is associated with increased anxiety, depression, and psychological distress.[2] The involuntary nature of puberty coupled with the emotional effects of changing hormones already present unprecedented challenges to your child. The continued application of harsh parenting in this context is as insensitive as it is ineffective.

If your personal parenting style is harsh in nature, consider using these three softer approaches.

1. Make space for your child to talk about their feelings without judgment or comparison.
2. Provide educational support in the form of tutorials or written guidance so they can learn how to manage their menstrual bleeding and other pubertal symptoms.
3. Communicate calmly and without screaming or yelling if they forget to pack pads or leak through their clothing. Accidents and mistakes happen, especially during periods of adjustment like the early puberty years.

By being less harsh and more warm, you can improve distress symptoms, decrease conduct problems, and be a better supporter of your child's needs.

Harshness isn't the only parenting style shown to worsen adolescent mental health. A study conducted in Kenya and Nigeria found that mothers often used scare tactics in their response to puberty. One specific example included a mother telling her child she would get cancer if she had a boyfriend. She essentially said that the moment you sleep with your boyfriend, cancer enters your womb, destroys it, and leads to death. These fear-based tactics were shown to influence emotional responses in adolescents, potentially causing anxiety and distress. Another study showed that threatening behaviors like this communicate to children that the world is unsafe and people are unpredictable. This leads to worsened depressive symptoms, especially in adolescents who already have difficulty recognizing and understanding their own emotions.[3]

In my years of practice, I've personally witnessed the ineffectiveness of fear-based parenting and scare tactics. In addition to eroding parental-child trust, this style of parenting seeks to gain control via manipulation, exaggeration, and even lies. Instead of presenting a balanced view of risks and benefits that might help inform future decision-making, threatening parental behaviors present a skewed view focusing on rejection, abandonment, and punishment. This distortion of reality sabotages the adolescent decision-making process before it even begins. By presenting these negative outcomes as inevitabilities, parents essentially rob their child of their inherent agency and forfeit their opportunity to demonstrate how choices can either promote or degrade personal values.

Instead of scaring your child into submission, try explaining how their pubertal changes present a new array of complex decisions, opportunities, and consequences. Be honest about what emotional, social, and physical concerns you have and how you hope your child will conduct themselves in a way that promotes their safety, happiness, and well-being. Be transparent about how it is normal to have new feelings and attractions and offer appropriate ways to manage them.

While maternal responses have a significant effect on adolescent mental health, paternal responses also play a critical role. Paternal emotional support impacts depression and anxiety symptoms, with less paternal support correlating to increased depression and anxiety.[4] This means fathers and nonmenstruating parents are important sources of support as well.

Interestingly, American adolescents report greater menstrual emotional and informational support when compared to other cultures, specifically Chinese, South Korean, and Japanese. While other cultures report high levels of tangible support (material or financial assistance), the emotional and informational support offered by American parents has a more significant impact on stress reduction in adolescents. In addition to cultural differences, financial differences are present as well. Lower socioeconomic groups have been shown to have less access to resources and information. For this reason, they tend to have less effective parental support, leading to increased distress as well as negative emotional responses. This means parental response is impacted by the degree of access to education and resources like this book.[5]

Conversely, parental response can have important positive impacts. Maternal comfort and support help to regulate how adolescents respond to social stress. When there is maternal support following social stressors, cortisol levels are reduced, leading to better stress recovery. Parental warmth and emotional support are associated with lower levels of anxiety and depressive symptoms. Effective parental support is especially critical in cases of early menarche, serving as a buffer to the associated long-term potential mental health issues and antisocial behavior.[6]

In summary, parental response can have positive or negative effects on a child's experience of puberty. These effects can be significant and long-lasting. Inadequate parental support, harsh parenting, fear tactics, secrecy, shame, and lack of information all lead to poorer outcomes. Warmth, emotional support, and provision of information all lead to positive outcomes. The most vulnerable to parental response are those who develop earlier and have earlier onset of menarche. Because of their increased social stress, potential for mental health issues, and antisocial behavior, their pubertal experience depends more heavily on adequate, intentional, and effective parental support.

Puberty is inevitable, but your child's experience of it is not. Their impressionability during this time truly means that you have the unique opportunity to shape their experience. Your response can promote confidence, resilience, and reassurance or evoke distress, shame, and fear. One day, your child may tell the story of their puberty experience to a stranger, colleague, or friend. Make sure that story is a good one.

8

Teaching the Things You Had to Learn the Hard Way

Showing Your Child How to Live in the World as a Menstruator

"Now what brings you two back in today?" I asked my former patient and her mom warmly. It was always nice to see familiar faces.

"She stinks," her mom said. When I failed to respond to her declaration, she shrugged her shoulders and added, "It is true! I should know. I'm her mom. I live with her every day, and I smell her. She stinks, and I'd rather tell her before someone else does."

I was mortified for her daughter.

I'd seen Kinsey nearly a year ago when she'd just started getting her period. Her periods were irregular at the time but had improved without any need for further evaluation. This was her first visit since. I noticed she seemed different. She wasn't as vibrant and carefree as she once was. She used to smile and wave to every person in the office, asking them about their day and complimenting them on their outfits. But today she sat quiet and withdrawn.

I turned in my seat to face her more directly. “Hi, Kinsey,” I said.

“Hey,” she replied. She looked embarrassed and defeated.

“Can you tell me your thoughts on why you’re here today?” I asked.

“My mom says I have a smell sometimes, and it is a bad smell that’s not normal or clean,” she said.

“And what do *you* think?” I asked.

“I don’t know. I don’t really smell anything, but sometimes kids at school say it too.”

I nodded. “How does that make you feel?”

Kinsey just shook her head and began to cry. “I’m sorry,” she said.

“It is okay. You do not need to apologize to me. This room is a safe place. It is safe for you to say what you need to and feel what you need to. So you do not need to say sorry for that. Okay?”

“Okay,” she replied.

We went ahead and did a physical exam. Kinsey didn’t have any abnormal vaginal discharge or signs of a vaginal source of odor. She just had body odor in the typical regions of her underarms and groin area. It wasn’t terribly offensive or abnormal. She was just a teenager who probably needed to improve her bathing and deodorant routine. But she was internalizing the identity of someone who stinks and carrying the feelings of anxiety and isolation that come with it.

Her mom’s belief that pointing out Kinsey’s body odor wouldn’t upset her was wrong. Yes, her mother needed to acknowledge the odor, but how she did it and the words she used mattered to Kinsey.

I talked with Kinsey and her mom about how different things were from last year. Kinsey had eczema and was previously advised by her dermatologist to avoid taking hot showers or showering too frequently. She used to take a shower every other day to avoid aggravating her eczema and had no issue. Now that she had more body odor, that plan needed to be modified. Kinsey also shared that the deodorant her mom bought her burned her underarms when she applied it. She had sensitive skin, and the strong deodorant was just too much for her to handle. Lastly, she still had some difficulty remembering to change her period pad while in school. It wasn't because she didn't know how or didn't want to. It was because she just forgot.

All these things were contributing to increased body odor, and they all had reasonable and fairly simple solutions. We made a plan that included lukewarm showers every day with an antibacterial soap for her underarms and groin area. We planned to moisturize immediately after showering to minimize the likelihood of eczema flares. We found a moisturizing deodorant for sensitive skin that didn't burn. It required her to reapply midday for continued odor protection, but she didn't mind because it didn't irritate her skin. And during her period, we planned to have her change her pad as soon as she got to lunch. If she also changed her pad right before school and right when she got home, she would be at low risk for leaks or odor.

Kinsey didn't need to be shamed; she needed strategies and support. All these changes were new to her, and her sensitive skin and eczema made them more challenging. By being curious about her needs, solution oriented, and patient, we finally got her to a place of comfort and confidence. It just took a little bit of effort and time.

If you've never been a menstruating middle schooler, this patient's experience may be entirely new to you. If you were once a menstruating middle schooler, Kinsey's situation may sound very familiar. Regardless, in order to be patient with your child, you will need to develop a sense of their current reality. You'll need to consider what they were once responsible for, what their hygiene practices previously consisted of, and how in tune they previously had to be with their body. Then consider how drastically those things change in puberty.

Studies show that it can take two years for adolescents to adjust to and become comfortable with menstruation. This makes sense because they aren't just adjusting physically; they are making significant emotional and social adjustments as well.[1] Parental support plays an important role in the adjustment process. For example, low perceived family support during menstruation has been shown to be associated with higher levels of anxiety, stress, and depression in adolescents. Adequate parental support can mitigate psychological distress and potentially help to shorten the adjustment period. Additionally, supportive parent-adolescent relationships have been shown to be critical for emotional regulation, impacting how well your child may cope with new experiences like menstruation.[2] So the work doesn't end when the first period ends. Continued support with practical guidance and patience is necessary for two years or more. Here are specific areas where they will need your help.

Personal Hygiene

The profound impact puberty has on personal hygiene is primarily due to the introduction of four key things: body hair, body odor, acne, and blood. Consideration of these new elements informs how we must approach implementation of an effective personal hygiene routine.

The first thing to consider is your unique child. The effectiveness of their hygiene routine will depend heavily on variables such as their daily schedule, attention to detail, involvement in sports, personal style, and more. We'll discuss a low-maintenance and general routine that you can customize according to the unique needs and desires of your own child.

Body Hair

Body hair is normal. The presence of body hair does not define hygiene status. For example, underarm hair isn't unhygienic. The removal of hair under the arms, on the legs, in the pubic area, and even on the face is a matter of preference rather than a matter of hygiene. However, the presence of hair in these places is associated with increased oil production, potential for issues like ingrown hairs, and a need for more intentional cleansing practices.

If hair removal is desired, safe and appropriate methods should be used. Shaving of legs and underarms should be done using a clean razor and shaving gel or cream. Hair removal on the face can easily be done with a specialized electric hair trimmer. These trimmers are compact and typically have protective engineering that make cuts unlikely and shaving gel unnecessary. For removal of pubic hair, shaving with a razor increases risks of irritation, folliculitis, and ingrown hairs. Use of depilatory creams should be done with caution because they can also cause irritation as well as contact dermatitis on sensitive skin like the pubic area and even the face. For an adolescent, trimming with scissors or using an electric trimmer may be easier.

Some parents don't allow body hair removal prior to a certain age. Some forbid hair removal entirely. Concerns vary from risk of self-injury to impact on self-esteem and even implications of sexual activity. The concerns are heightened when discussing the removal of pubic hair. A study evaluating the attitudes and practices of hair removal in adolescents ages twelve to twenty years old found that 70 percent of adolescents reported routinely shaving or removing pubic hair. Although pubic hair removal was more commonly seen in adolescents who were sexually active, the most significant influences on whether an adolescent chose to remove pubic hair were friends and family. This means that most adolescents choose to remove body hair due to social influences, not sexual ones.[3]

If your child wants to remove body hair, it is important to speak with them about why. The majority of the time, you'll find their desire to be related to influences of friends, family, teammates, and peers. Avoidance of hair removal discussions does not prevent experimentation and may inadvertently lead to unsafe unsupervised attempts. It is important to work with your child to come up with a plan that supports their physical and emotional well-being, is safe, and is consistent with personal values. It may take a few tries before finding the hair removal method that works best, which is why patience and understanding are key.

Body Odor

Body odor in puberty may be one of the more challenging adjustments children have to make. Your child could previously bathe once per day, rub on some lotion, and feel fresh as a daisy. Now, their body is producing increased perspiration, and odor-causing bacteria are turning their sweat into offensive smells. The first line of defense against body odor is daily bathing. Daily bathing can be done at night or in the morning but should be done with soap and warm water. Antibacterial soap can be especially effective at reducing the amount of odor-causing bacteria on the skin. For the child who is active in sports or who is consistently active enough to break a sweat, daily bathing may not be sufficient. After intense physical exercise, an extra shower may be necessary to remove dirt, oil, and sweat and to control odors.

The secondary defense against odor is the use of deodorant. While there are numerous types of deodorant available, a general practice is to start with gentle deodorant first and then step up in strength as needed. Gentle deodorant is that which is fragrance-free, undyed, and hypoallergenic. While deodorant is very commonly used, certain ingredients can irritate skin, and certain fragrances can be intolerable for those with sensitive skin. Daily use of deodorant, especially under the arms, is recommended. All-over body deodorant is also an option but should be used with caution. If irritation or intolerance occurs, it should be discontinued immediately.

Acne

The presence of acne is not a sign of poor hygiene or uncleanliness. Over 85 percent of teens will have acne at some point. Despite how common it is, acne can be one of the most challenging parts of puberty. Acne can significantly impact self-esteem, well-being, mental health, and quality of life. Untreated severe acne can lead to scarring and disfigurement.[4] For these reasons, acne should not be dismissed or reduced to just cosmetics. If it is seriously affecting your child, it should be addressed and taken seriously.

General hygiene for acne prevention and management includes cleansing the face twice per day. It is typically recommended to begin with a gentle over-the-counter facial cleanser. If this isn't sufficient, use of a cleaner with salicylic acid may be more effective. If this doesn't help, use of benzoyl peroxide may be a better option. Acne that persists despite the consistent use of over-the-counter options should be evaluated by a medical professional. Prescription-strength acne treatments can be very effective and can drastically improve the self-esteem and quality of life of your child.

Acne can worsen just before menstruation and can fluctuate throughout the pubertal years. Acne management often requires trial and error, and it can take two to three months to see improvement with different methods. For these reasons, successful acne management requires partnership, consistency, and patience.

Leak Prevention and Management

Leaks are an inevitability of menstruation, but that doesn't make them any less annoying or frustrating. While most people improve their prevention of leaks over time, you are never too experienced, too old, or too good to leak. Unlike with the bladder or rectum, there is no expectation or possibility of control over leakage of blood from the vagina. Because the uterus doesn't have a sphincter that loosens and tightens to start or stop blood flow, there is no voluntary mechanism of command. We are always at the mercy of our own random, fluctuating, inconsistent flow.

One of the first techniques to master for leak prevention is optimal pad placement. It may seem intuitive, but pad placement isn't as simple as one might think. For shorter pads, pad placement is critical to leak prevention. Placement too far forward or too far back can easily lead to leaks. It's important to inform your child that optimal pad placement can change depending on the time of day. If they are headed to school in the morning and will be sitting upright and walking a lot, they should place their pad more forward in their underwear. The easiest way to do this is to identify the double-lined portion in the center and shift the pad slightly forward in relation to that area. In the evening and before bed, they may need to place the pad farther back in their underwear. This is important for sleeping, especially if they tend to sleep on their back or side. When they sleep on their back, they may leak beyond their pad if it isn't placed far enough back. When they sit or stand, they can leak in front of their pad if it's not shifted far enough forward. When using a pad, understanding anatomy and body positioning is key. The vaginal opening is not located where your labia begin or originate from. It is farther back and closer to where the labia end or terminate. Your pad must be placed accordingly.

Another important skill is product selection. More specifically, you cannot start with a product that was never intended to handle your flow. For example, with a heavier period flow, a panty liner is a nonstarter. Additionally, many heavy bleeders will never use a light tampon in their lives. If your child has to change their product more often than once per hour, they should step up in absorbency. If they cannot increase absorbency, they may need to use a dual product approach.

One of the best approaches for leak prevention is the appropriate use of more than one product. On heavier days, some menstruators could use a regular tampon and a pad for backup. Some preteens prefer to use a pad with period underwear as their second line of defense. Others may try a menstrual cup or disc with period underwear as backup. In rare situations of heavier flow, I've seen people use two pads overlapping each other for better coverage. If there's concern for excessive bleeding, it is important to seek prompt medical evaluation. If there isn't a concern for heavy bleeding, know that strategic product utilization is a major help in preventing leaks.

Finally, when leaks occur, take the following steps to remove stains. Try to blot any stains first to remove any excess blood. Next, rinse the item in cold water to lift the stain. With detergent, spot clean the area using gentle scrubbing/rubbing until the stain is gone. Once done, wash as usual. This is especially useful to remove stains from underwear, clothes, and bedsheets. Other helpful steps would be to consider using darker sheets or wearing clothes that don't visibly stain as easily. Many people have underwear they only use when they are on their period, even if it is not specifically period underwear.

Again, leaks and stains happen. They are inevitable due to the nature of period blood flow. Try not to look at stains as personal failures or signs of immaturity. Have patience and offer support. With time and practice, leaks will become less frequent.

Product Disposal

When my mom first taught me how to dispose of my used period products, I thought her approach was excessive. I was taught to wrap my products in tissue, place them in a small garbage bag, tie it up, and place it into the larger outdoor garbage bin. While this felt like overkill at the time, it ensured proper disposal of products and prevented them from falling out of the too-small trash can in our bathroom. It also helped to prevent odors that can occur when material saturated with blood is left out for an extended period of time.

Product disposal can be a point of frustration because it requires some decent preplanning and attention to detail. One easy method of product disposal is to use the packaging of the new product to wrap and dispose of the old product. This works best for pads and liners. Alternatively, your child can wrap the used product in toilet paper and dispose of it in the designated containers. Disposal can be challenging when there's no trash can available, the designated container is full, or the product is very saturated. A good backup option is for your child to keep a plastic bag in their purse or backpack where they can put their used product until they can get to a proper location to dispose of it.

In your home and in the homes of friends and family, proper disposal is important when pets and small children are present. Because either could find themselves exploring low and uncovered trash cans, take extra care to properly dispose of used products in these settings.

Proper product disposal is not something we discuss to suggest that period blood is dirty, offensive, or distasteful. It is, however, an important part of menstrual management and warrants guidance.

Period Tracking

What period tracking lacks in excitement, it makes up for in usefulness. Many people think of cycle tracking as a tool related to pregnancy only: It is either for those who are trying to get pregnant or those trying to avoid pregnancy. But its utility extends well beyond that.

I encourage all menstruators to track their periods. From the very first period, tracking is an important part of period management. With the help of modern technology, many preteens and teens conveniently track their periods right on their phones. There are countless period tracking apps that boast a variety of features from upcoming period reminders to past cycle data summaries and even fertile window alerts. I'm most impressed by apps that offer medically accurate education, ensure data privacy, and contribute to research that improves our understanding of menstruation. Despite their clever marketing, from a user standpoint, their standard functions are quite similar. They take the data you provide, store it, and make predictions based on it. In fact, nearly everything the apps do for you can be done using a paper calendar and a pen.

Period tracking is simply the documentation of menstruation from the first day of bleeding to the last day of bleeding. This tells us the length of the period or the length of menstruation. The average period length is five days, with a normal period lasting seven days or less. When this is done sequentially, a pattern arises that shows the length of the menstrual cycle. Your menstrual cycle is calculated from day one of one period to day one of the very next period. For adolescents, the normal menstrual cycle length is between twenty-one days and forty-five days. If we know our typical menstrual cycle length, we can use estimates to predict when our next period will begin. But there's much more that we can do.

Period tracking is one of the simplest ways to determine whether the basic characteristics of our cycle are normal. Periods that last too many days should be discussed with your medical provider, and periods that occur too frequently or too infrequently warrant evaluation as well. Period tracking also highlights an important misconception among many menstruators.

Many people believe that their period is supposed to start on the same day each month, meaning "I usually get my period on the fifth" or "mine comes on the twenty-first." This misconception that your period arrives with respect to a calendar date is false. Your uterus doesn't have a calendar, and your ovaries have no idea what date it is. Because months have varying numbers of days, it is normal and expected that your period will start on different dates each month. Moreover, if your cycle length is longer than thirty-one days, you may go a full calendar month without having a period. This would be totally normal for you and should not be cause for alarm. Conversely, if your cycle length is shorter than twenty-eight days, you will inevitably have two periods within the same month. This does not represent an abnormality and shouldn't cause alarm either.

Period tracking is so important because it is the best way to get the most accurate information about your own body. It allows you to determine your personal "normal," which can't be captured by a singular calendar date. It also allows us to have a baseline for reference when concerns or changes occur.

In the absence of irregularity or change, period tracking can still be super useful to the average adolescent. When they track their period, they can better predict when their next period will start. This can help them plan. If they have period cramps, they can get ahead of the pain by taking medication early. They can modify their diet leading up to their period to avoid inflammatory foods that might make their period pain worse. They can pack a heating pad in their luggage or pack period-friendly outfits or even extra underwear. Period tracking helps them plan, and planning helps them succeed.

Even the best and most attentive person may have trouble with period tracking when they first start. Initially, it may not seem important, feasible, or worthwhile. But that's why parental support is necessary. In the beginning, it is helpful if you partner with your child in tracking their period. For younger menstruators, it may be necessary to track their cycle along with them. For older and more responsible menstruators, you may just need to remind them to track it. Remember this is a task that your child has never had to keep up with in their life. Your patience, encouragement, and guidance will make all the difference.

Period Kit Packing

One of the most helpful tips for managing periods is to create and maintain a well-stocked period kit. A period kit is a collection of all the essential period care items. Period kits can be kept in cars, sports bags, school lockers, and even at home. They should be customized to the user, considering their flow, comfort, activities, and typical symptoms.

For example, an eleven-year-old who has mild period pain, has moderate period flow, doesn't use tampons, and plays softball may need the following: period underwear, some medium flow pads, an extra uniform bottom, an over-the-counter pain reliever, water, hand sanitizer, and personal cleansing wipes.

A thirteen-year-old dancer with light periods and no period pain and who gets moderate acne around her period and splits her time evenly between her parents' homes may need two period kits. She may need light and regular tampons, a few light pads and panty liners, an extra pair of underwear, and a pack of pimple patches.

A fourteen-year-old avid reader with heavy periods, moderate period pain, and menstrual headaches may need the following: menstrual discs, heavy flow pads, heating patches, over-the-counter pain reliever, extra underwear, an extra pair of pants, personal cleansing wipes, and their favorite book.

You can customize a period kit with whatever your child wants or needs during their period. The kit is meant to provide comfort, relieve pain, avoid leaks, and reduce stress. Period kits are especially helpful to have for menstruators who are still getting used to predicting their next cycle, packing their necessary supplies, and managing their flow. With the help of your organization, preparation, and patience, your child can always be ready for what may come.

9

More Than Birth Control

Understanding the Role of Hormones as Medicine

A sticky note with the words "Please call Dad back" was on my desk after lunch. I wanted more context, but the only other details noted were two letters, which I took to be the patient's initials, and the nine numbers that made up the patient's medical record number.

I typed in the number and remembered the visit as soon as I read her name. "Oh, Esther," I said aloud.

I had seen Esther in my office earlier that week with both of her parents. It's rare to get both parents at once because most parents aren't clamoring to take their teen to the gynecologist. In fact, when I do see dads, it is almost always because the mom couldn't make it. In this case, Esther's mom was there, and she was very present, capable, and aware. Even so, it was clear that the authority in their family lay with the father.

Esther came to see me with complaints of monthly physical and emotional symptoms that preceded her period each month. She noted breast tenderness, cramping, and nausea but also had significant mood swings with irritability and tearfulness. Her mom felt sorry for her. Her father seemed a bit skeptical. He asked a lot of questions, but I didn't mind. It was refreshing to see a father so present and involved in his daughter's health and well-being. We reviewed a PMS questionnaire together, and Esther met the criteria for an official diagnosis, but before we could complete the visit, her father had to leave to go to work.

When I presented the options for treatment of her PMS to Esther and her mom, they reported already trying the recommended lifestyle modifications. They ultimately chose to try hormonal therapy. The hormonal therapy chosen was a low-dose progesterone-only contraceptive pill. I'd prescribed the pills only a few days ago, so I doubted Esther had even had time to start taking them, let alone have additional questions about them.

I knew I had to wait for my conversation with Esther's father to know for sure, but I had a good idea what the issue would be.

"You put my daughter on *birth control*?" he asked.

"Well, I wouldn't put it that way, but I suppose technically—"

"She doesn't need birth control. She's not having sex!" he interrupted.

I let him finish.

"We came to you so you could help her with her periods, not give her birth control pills. I thought I liked you and that you were doing respectful and important work for girls like my Esther, but this is just shameful."

This was not the first time I had offended a parent by prescribing hormonal contraception and wouldn't be the last. I'd been explaining myself to concerned parents for years at that point, and my argument was always the same. The appropriateness of medication isn't determined by societal stigma; it is determined by medical indication. Esther needed medication to help with her PMS because her symptoms were bothersome to her and not improved by nonpharmacological methods. She'd tried magnesium, vitamin B6, and calcium. She already used a heating pad, drank ginger tea, and tried over-the-counter options. She had elected to try prescribed medication because what she had already tried wasn't working. I'd explained all this to her mom, and I was sure she'd already told her husband exactly what I was about to say, but I figured he needed to hear it from me to believe it.

"I understand your concern, and I'd like to explain my reasoning if that's okay," I said.

"Please!" he replied.

"Esther met the diagnostic criteria for premenstrual syndrome or PMS. The symptoms she's been complaining of for the past several months are all consistent with this diagnosis. There are many ways to treat PMS that do not include birth control, but she has tried those already. In her case, this medication is indicated. While she may not be sexually active, she doesn't have to be to benefit from the numerous noncontraceptive benefits of birth control. Because

PMS is due to her body's response to hormonal fluctuations around her period, it makes sense that hormonal medication would be one of the best methods to improve this."

"Okay, I'm hearing you," he said.

"You know how some people use Tylenol to treat fevers and others may use it to treat headaches?"

"Yeah," he answered.

"Hormonal contraception or birth control is the same way. Some people use it to prevent pregnancy, and that's a really important use. But other people, like your daughter, use it to help with their PMS. You don't have to have a fever to take Tylenol just because it is one of its more common uses, right? So for Esther, we chose the medicine with benefits most likely to address her specific needs. That's the definition of appropriate, and there's no shame in that."

He later thanked me for taking the time to explain everything to him and gave his wife the approval to fill the prescription. Esther returned for her follow-up appointment a few months later. She'd already seen significant improvement in her PMS symptoms as well as in her overall quality of life.

When many parents hear the words "birth control," they are immediately alarmed. Their minds start to recall every negative piece of misinformation or horror story they've ever seen, heard, or read. That's partly why I prefer the term "hormonal therapy." It is less upsetting and more accurate, especially when using these medications for their well-established noncontraceptive benefits. Because of the role that our hormones play in menstruation, hormonal therapy can help with many symptoms that have nothing to do with pregnancy prevention. This means their utility and appropriate use extends beyond patients who are sexually active. Hormonal therapy can be used to manage period pain as well as heavy bleeding, irregular bleeding, severe acne, unwanted hair growth, PMS, PMDD, endometriosis, polycystic ovary syndrome, and more.

Hormonal therapy is also sometimes used to help treat patients with seizure disorders. It is estimated that up to 60 percent of menstruators with epilepsy experience worsening of seizures during certain phases of the menstrual cycle. This is called catamenial epilepsy and is thought to be due to the fact that the hormones that regulate the menstrual cycle—estrogen and progesterone—impact the excitability of neurons, or the cells of the brain and nervous system. While progesterone has been shown to have anti-seizure effects, estrogen has been shown to increase seizures. In combination with traditional seizure medications, hormonal birth control, specifically the progesterone-based options, can be used to achieve better seizure control for these patients.[1] Sadly, many of them are unaware of this important option.

Another lesser-known use for hormonal therapy is the suppression and treatment of menstruation symptoms in children and teens with autism spectrum disorder (ASD). For some of these children, the experience of menstruation and bleeding is terribly distressing. This is especially the case for children with heightened sensory sensitivities and emotional regulation and communication challenges. Many parents and caregivers of menstruators with ASD don't even know this option exists. They often believe menstruation is something they must endure, not something that can be managed medically.

Hormonal therapy is best described as medication that is very similar to the hormones produced by the ovaries: estrogen and progesterone. These two hormones typically rise and fall in a cyclical manner to cause thickening of the uterine lining, ovulation, and menstruation. Hormonal therapy provides these hormones in a more consistent and steady dose. When this steady dose prevents ovulation, it prevents pregnancy. Prevention of ovulation can also help to reduce the formation of ovarian cysts, which can be helpful for adolescents who tend to produce ovarian cysts or experience cyst rupture and related pain. Many hormonal therapies also prevent the uterine lining from thickening as much as it usually would. This thinner uterine lining can lead to lighter periods or even cessation of periods, which can be helpful for adolescents who have heavy bleeding and may suffer from anemia. Additionally, many hormonal therapies significantly reduce period cramps and pain.

To better understand hormonal therapy options, it is helpful to note that there are only two categories: those with estrogen and progesterone and those with progesterone alone. Those with both estrogen and progesterone, or the combination options, include pills, a transdermal patch, and a vaginal ring. Progesterone-only options include pills, an injection, an arm implant, and an IUD.

Pills are prescribed with daily dosing and require the most effort for appropriate use. They also give the user the most control and are the easiest to discontinue. The transdermal patch is applied weekly and can be a good option for someone who wants control but doesn't want to have to remember a daily medication. The vaginal ring is inserted monthly and is the longest-acting method of the combination options.

The injection is administered every three months and is the most difficult to discontinue because it has to be metabolized and cannot just be removed. The arm implant and IUD are considered to be long-acting reversible contraception because they are effective for a number of years once inserted. Although initially approved for three years, the arm implant may be effective for five years. The hormonal IUD may be effective for up to eight years.

People with sensitivity or contraindications to estrogen should use progesterone-only options. Because there are several different health conditions that might preclude the use of estrogen, it is important to discuss your unique risks with your qualified medical provider.

Parents have a lot of concerns about hormonal therapy, especially when prescribing to adolescents. One prevalent concern is that the provision of hormonal therapy that is also effective as contraception might increase or encourage early sexual activity. Contraception use even for pregnancy prevention is not correlated with increased sexual activity. It is, however, associated with a reduction in unintended pregnancies. Parents may also worry that hormonal therapy might decrease future fertility. This is simply not true. Numerous studies have shown that hormonal contraception does not negatively impact future fertility.

METHOD	PROGESTIN	PROGESTIN + ESTROGEN
Pill	Mini Pill	Combined Oral Contraceptives (COCs) (e.g., ethinyl estradiol + levonorgestrel)
Injection	Depo-Provera (medroxyprogesterone)	Not available as a combined injection
Implant	Nexplanon (etonogestrel)	No combined implant available
Intrauterine Device (IUD)	Mirena, Kyleena, Skyla, Liletta (levonorgestrel)	No combined hormonal IUD available
Patch	No progestin-only patch	Xulane, Twirla (ethinyl estradiol + norelgestromin)
Vaginal Ring		NuvaRing, Annovera (ethinyl estradiol + etonogestrel / segesterone acetate)

Additionally, there can be concerns around increased risk for blood clots in the deep veins of the body. This risk is primarily related to estrogen and is thereby noted with combined hormonal therapy options. Progesterone-only options (other than the injection) are not felt to increase clotting risk. The risk is highest in the first year of use and after restarting hormonal therapy after at least a month of discontinuation. While the risk of blood clots in combined hormonal therapy users is higher than in nonusers, it's significantly less than the risk in pregnancy and postpartum. The risk of clotting is highest in those who are obese, have clotting disorders, have a strong family history of blood clots, or are over thirty-five or smokers.[2]

Another very valid concern is related to cancer risk. While studies have shown a very minimal increased risk of breast cancer, hormonal contraceptive use is associated with an overall reduction in cancer risk. This is because it is associated with a decreased risk in ovarian, endometrial, and colorectal cancers. The significant reduction in risk of these cancers outweighs the minimal increased risk in breast cancer.

Hormonal therapy is not the answer for every period symptom, and it isn't the best option for every menstruator. As with any medication, there are risks and benefits that need to be weighed on an individual basis and in accordance with personal values and comfort levels. However, a general understanding of how hormonal therapy works and what conditions it might be used to treat is important. We cannot necessarily predict which child will have debilitating pain, heavy bleeding, or severe PMS. When these conditions arise, we must consider every available option until we find the one that is safe and effective. Our children deserve to have relief from bothersome period symptoms, and we shouldn't let unsubstantiated fears keep them from receiving the help they need.

Hormonal therapy has been improved and studied thoroughly over the last few decades, with proven safety and efficacy for many noncontraceptive indications. Whether used for contraception or not, they are medications that allow many people with periods to live a life with greater comfort, control, and freedom. They are appropriate to use when they're medically indicated, not just when they are socially acceptable. Don't limit your child's options based on your limited thinking. For many menstruators, hormonal therapy is way more than just birth control.

It may be what controls their bleeding so they no longer have fainting spells and headaches from severe anemia. It might be what has reduced their likelihood of seizures so they can finally travel with their family. It might be the only thing that has improved their period pain so they can continue to play the sport they love. It might be the best option for treating their PMS so they can stay focused and engaged in their competitive college classes. Whatever the need may be, if it can be safely and effectively addressed with hormonal therapy, the use is valid. There is no need for popular opinion, majority vote, or spectator commentary. It's your child. It's their life. And they deserve to live it fully.

10

How to Recognize Abnormal Symptoms Early

It was one of the lowest blood levels I'd ever seen. It was so low that the lab thought it was an error. When it was unchanged on the repeat check, we were all shocked. But no one was more shocked than our patient's mom.

Her daughter had started getting periods about a year ago, and they had established a simple system. The mom would keep the cabinet stocked with pads, and the daughter would get them when she needed them. The last time they'd even talked about her period was a year ago when she first started menstruating. So her mom hadn't noticed when her daughter returned to the cabinet multiple times per day for three months straight due to prolonged bleeding. She hadn't noticed when the color slowly drained from her daughter's skin and her breaths became quicker. She didn't notice she'd been more tired and had been having more headaches than usual.

She didn't notice until the morning when her daughter collapsed while trying to tie her shoes. So she sat in the emergency room in disbelief as we worked to transfuse bag after bag of blood to replace what had been lost.

They stayed in the hospital for three days while her daughter received medication to stop the bleeding. Once her bleeding stopped and her blood count improved, she would be able to go home.

When it was time for the daughter to be discharged, her mom finally asked, "How do we make sure this doesn't happen again?"

My answer was simple. "You've got to pay really close attention to her, and you have to check in."

For this patient, a simple and regular check-in might have shortened her suffering and saved her from a blood transfusion. But many parents don't realize just how important it is to continue to regularly assess the mental, physical, and emotional well-being of their child. Getting your child through the first stages of puberty and their first period is a major victory and should be celebrated. It is not, however, your cue to check out. In fact, it is the perfect time to master the art of checking in.

Many people let their guard down when it comes to periods because they are natural. They assume that a normal and natural process like menstruation can't possibly cause harm or become abnormal. Much like natural disasters, the natural aspect of periods doesn't exempt them from extremes. These can be extremes of bleeding, pain, or even mood. For an adolescent, it may be challenging to recognize or promptly report changes, especially if they aren't sure where normal ends and where abnormal begins.

The initial step in the check-in phase is education. Reinforce the foundational points that will help your child identify concerning changes. Remind them that period pain is common but not necessarily normal. Pain that either worsens or prevents them from doing their regular activities needs to be evaluated. Sudden and intense pain is the most concerning, especially if it is associated with nausea and vomiting. If they experience severe pain, they need to let you know immediately. They should not try to increase medicine doses without your permission. They should not take medicine from friends or peers, especially if it is not clearly labeled or in an unopened individual package. If they have pain that can be treated with over-the-counter medication, you can document it and make an appointment with their doctor. If the pain is severe and not relieved by medication, they need more prompt evaluation.

Severe pain raises concern for endometriosis. Endometriosis is a medical diagnosis where tissue similar to the uterine lining is abnormally located outside the uterus. It is often characterized by significant pain and requires specialized care and management for the best results. They need to know that they are not expected to try to tough it out or push through.

You should also remind your child of normal bleeding patterns. A normal period should last seven days or less. A normal menstrual cycle should be no less than twenty-one days and no more than forty-five days from the first day of bleeding for one period to the first day of bleeding for the next period. It's concerning if they skip more than ninety days between periods. If they go too long without a period, there may be an underlying hormonal issue. The most common cause for prolonged missed periods is polycystic ovary syndrome, which affects 10 percent of people with periods and is diagnosed through medical evaluation. It is associated with other issues like weight gain, excessive facial and body hair, and severe acne. It has associated risks that include diabetes, cardiovascular disease, and infertility. For this reason, early diagnosis is key.

It is also important to diagnose anemia early. Anemia occurs when the body doesn't have enough red blood cells to get oxygen to all the vital organs of the body as effectively as it should. There are many causes of anemia, but anemia related to periods is typically due to bleeding too long or too often. Bleeding lasting longer than seven days or cycles shorter than twenty-one days are a risk for losing too much blood. When you are anemic, your heart must work harder to circulate your blood. If left untreated, this could lead to heart failure. Anemia is associated with symptoms like fatigue, headaches, lightheadedness/dizziness, and pallor. Mild anemia can resolve without treatment as long as the source of blood loss is controlled. Anemia that is more severe may warrant iron therapy to help in the production of new red blood cells. Anemia that is very severe may require a blood transfusion.

Because of the immaturity of the HPO axis, young menstruators are at high risk for irregular bleeding in the one to three years after menarche. During this time, bleeding check-ins are very important. They are most effective when period tracking is being used regularly. For this reason, be sure to remind your child of the importance of tracking their periods. If they are unable to track their own periods for any reason, consider doing it for them.

Another bleeding characteristic to check in about is the amount of blood. While it is normal for period blood flow to vary throughout your days of bleeding, it should be noted if there is too much bleeding too quickly. It is possible to have a normal menstrual cycle length and normal duration of your period but still bleed too much and develop anemia. The general recommendation is to seek medical evaluation if you are bleeding through a period product in less than one hour or changing your period product more often than once per hour for more than two hours. Rapid blood loss can be seen in conditions like uterine fibroids, uterine polyps, rare cases of vascular abnormalities, and undiagnosed bleeding disorders. In fact, due to the onset of regular bleeding, menarche is a common time when new menstruators are diagnosed with bleeding disorders. Although they were most likely born with these disorders, the regular monthly bleeding revealed the underlying condition.

Period symptoms that you should check in about include nausea, vomiting, breast tenderness, and headaches. These physical symptoms in conjunction with mood symptoms like irritability and sadness can be signs of PMS. While it is estimated that three out of four of menstruators have experienced some symptoms of PMS, it can still be stressful and may benefit from treatment. PMS treatment depends on the symptoms experienced, but it is commonly managed with a combination of therapies including lifestyle changes, heat, NSAIDs, and hormonal therapy. When PMS becomes very severe and impairs daily function, it becomes known as premenstrual dysphoric disorder. PMDD is a debilitating condition that causes significant emotional and physical distress. It is also treated with a variety of medications but may require the use of antidepressant medication as well.

Many parents expect their menstruating child to experience mood changes, irritability, or even bloating and cramps, but it is important to pay attention to how these physical and mood changes affect your child. When they are bothered by these symptoms or severely impaired, it's time to take them for medical evaluation. Because of the emotional components of PMS and PMDD, it may be difficult for your child to effectively communicate what they're feeling. If you notice severe mood changes, don't assume defiance or dramatization. Consider PMS and PMDD. Timely diagnosis and treatment of these conditions can drastically improve well-being and quality of life.

Check-ins don't have to be tedious or awkward. They just need to occur regularly and be conducted effectively. When checking in, ask open-ended questions about mood, discomfort, and physical symptoms. Ask about bleeding, and review any period calendars or period tracking apps. Observe your child for any signs of sickness, physical distress, or loss of color. Be attentive when you speak with them, and listen for any signs of hopelessness, sorrow, irritability, anxiety, or depression. Pay attention to their sleep habits, their food intake, and online use. And finally, if they report a concern to you, believe them. Believe that they are overwhelmed, depressed, in too much pain, or unable to focus. Believe them, offer support, and then get them the evaluation they need.

11

Acknowledge and Treat Pain

"What can I say? She's her mother's child."

I didn't understand the statement.

I'd just told my thirteen-year-old patient, Marie, that I was concerned about her abnormal periods and wanted to evaluate her bleeding and pain with blood tests and imaging studies. My hope was to find a diagnosis to better inform a treatment plan, but her mom seemed to be drawing a different conclusion.

"This is how it starts, sweetheart," she continued, grabbing her daughter's hand. "They will do test after test after test and never find a thing."

"Has that been your experience?" I asked her.

"Oh yes! Since I can remember! So when she turned eleven, I told her to get ready, because her periods were going to be god-awful! All the women in my family have terrible periods. It is how we're made. My doctor never could figure it out, and he told me to learn to live with it."

"Oh wow. I'm so sorry. Do you still struggle with terrible periods?"

"No, dear! I have made it to menopause and couldn't be happier. I'll take hot flashes over periods any day. As far as I'm concerned, the only good thing to ever come from my uterus was this girl right here. Otherwise, it has been a hellhole. It sucks. I know it," she said, turning to Marie. "But at least your mama can understand your pain." She patted her daughter's thigh.

The look on Marie's face said she didn't find this to be anywhere near as comforting as her mother intended it to be.

"What if I told you we don't want Marie to just suffer? What if I said my job is to find a treatment plan that improves her quality of life well before she hits menopause?"

Marie's mom had experienced severe period symptoms. This experience likely caused her to feel isolated, frustrated, and helpless. When she was unable to find relief and doctors were unable to find a diagnosis, she coped with humor. She decided to rebrand her lack of diagnosis as being undiagnosable. She reframed her misfortune as a novelty and her years in pain as a badge of honor. This approach allowed her to avoid the awkwardness of others' sympathy and the embarrassment of their pity. She formed the belief that period pain was her fate and one that was best fought with humor-based acceptance. So when Marie began to have periods, she eagerly prepared her for the worst instead of advocating for effective medical management and finding ways to comfort her.

I talked with them about the steps I planned to take to evaluate Marie's pain. I talked about how an ultrasound was a great tool to evaluate the reproductive structures, but a normal ultrasound did not rule out the presence of all conditions or causes. I discussed how endometriosis can run in families and often can't be seen on ultrasound. I also talked extensively about options.

I discussed over-the-counter treatments and strategies for optimal dosing. I discussed nonpharmacological options like supplements, heat, exercise, rest, and yoga. I also discussed prescribed medications like anti-inflammatory medicines and hormonal therapy. By the time I finished, both Marie and her mom had renewed hope in the possibility of a future that wasn't dominated by pain.

"There are tons of options available, and I won't quit until we find the one that works best for your daughter," I told her.

After trying several options, we decided to try surgical intervention. During a noninvasive surgery, we collected biopsies and removed tissue that was confirmed to be endometriosis. Because I suspected this, I had obtained consent to place a hormonal IUD while she was under anesthesia. We were able to do a procedure that gave us a diagnosis as well as treatment, all at the same time.

Months later, Marie's pain was so improved that her mother could hardly believe it. Although she still had some pain, her life wasn't ruled by it, and she didn't have to wait for relief until she got a hysterectomy or went into menopause. She got to experience her relief as a teen because her pain was taken seriously and she learned that treatment was possible.

Most people have at least some pain with their period. While we tend to refer to period pain as "cramps," pain related to menstruation can take many forms. There are menstruators who have severe back pain, nausea, vomiting, headaches, breast tenderness, leg pain, pain with bowel movements, bladder pain, ovulation pain, and more. While period pain occurs commonly, that doesn't mean it is always normal. And even in the absence of an identifiable cause, it may still warrant treatment.

The trouble with pain is that it is invisible, incredibly complex, and nearly impossible to objectively measure. While there are external signs of pain that can be observed in how someone walks, sits, or even speaks, pain is not often noted unless it is communicated. Not only must we be able to communicate that we are in pain, we are also tasked with finding someone who will believe us. Unfortunately, this can be the more challenging task of the two.

There are several research studies that have demonstrated disparities in pain management based on sex. Female patients who present to emergency rooms for complaints of abdominal pain wait longer for pain medicine than male patients who report the same thing. Female patients are less likely than male patients to be prescribed pain medicine, with pain in females being underestimated more often. Another study revealed that when female patients reported their pain scores, those scores were 10 percent less likely to be recorded by nurses when compared to pain scores of males.

Furthermore, these pain biases are consistent across medical practitioners with both male and female physicians prescribing fewer pain-relieving medications to female patients.[1]

Provider bias is influenced by a number of gender stereotypes, most of which suggest that women are more likely to exaggerate their pain. One stereotype is that women are more likely to be emotionally expressive and thereby are more likely to dramatize their pain experiences. This stereotype leads to the belief that pain reports of women are less credible. In response, providers underestimate pain in female patients in a misguided attempt to correct for their "flawed" self-assessment. When providers actually do acknowledge the presence of pain, women are more likely to be prescribed psychological treatments rather than pain medications, meaning providers believe women are more likely to benefit from medicine that impacts their psychological perception of pain rather than the traditional route of analgesic pain therapy.[2]

As disheartening as it may be to learn of the extensive bias in pain treatment, it is important to note that this bias isn't limited to just the healthcare setting. For centuries, pain related to the uterus, vagina, cervix, and ovaries has been normalized. Not just period pain but also labor pain, vulvar pain, and IUD insertion pain have been considered to be normal and acceptable. As a society, we essentially believe that pain is deserving of sympathy and treatment unless that pain is in any way related to female reproductive health. Because of this societal normalization, the majority of young menstruators also believe that period pain is normal and should be endured or managed. This normalization of pain is often reinforced by mothers, aunts, sisters, other family members, and friends. As a result, menstruators are less likely to seek medical advice and more likely to use more private methods like self-care strategies and home remedies for pain.

Stigma around menstruation plays a significant role in the hesitancy of adolescents to discuss their menstrual pain. One study showed that many adolescents still believe that periods are taboo, gross, and associated with weakness.[3] This is especially the case in school where there is less knowledge about menstrual pain, less support, and increased social pressure to conform or fit in. Student athletes tend to hold themselves to higher and sometimes unrealistic standards that they should be able to push through their pain. Consequently, they may not report period pain because they fear their teammates and peers either won't understand or will express disapproval due to sports being equated to physical strength and endurance.

The fact is that our pain cannot be healed until our relationship with pain is. We have to unlearn the stereotypes that teach us period pain is trivial, unimportant, and unworthy of treatment. We have to reject the bias that says reports of pain are exaggerated or unreliable when they are made by a female patient or adolescent. We have to advocate for pain relief and adequate treatment even when we can't measure, see, or fully understand another person's pain. More importantly, we have to believe our children when they tell us they are in pain. Period pain is a physical symptom, but its impacts are far-reaching. It impacts the whole person, not just parts of them.

Period pain has been shown to impact physical functioning, daily functioning, and sleep. Physical functioning is impacted when a menstruator's ability to engage in their usual exercise and physical activity is limited by pain. Some people have to significantly modify their workouts, while others have to avoid exercise entirely. This may seem minor, but physical exercise has well-established mental health benefits that are critical to maintaining mood and emotional well-being. Daily functioning is affected by pain with menstruators being unable to stand for long periods at work or perform manual labor like lifting. Additionally, pain can impair concentration, focus, and productivity. This effect can be seen in school or at work with increased absenteeism. Period pain can also increase fatigue by negatively affecting sleep. Severe pain can interrupt overnight sleep, causing awakening and making it difficult for sleep to resume. This poor sleep quality results in fatigue that can impair school and work performance. Ultimately, severe pain is to blame for many lost hours and countless lost dollars.[4]

The psychological effects of period pain are also significant. Adolescents with severe period pain can begin to think negatively about their bodies, feeling abnormal and physically flawed. This thought process impairs body image and can worsen self-esteem. Period pain can impact anxiety by causing persistent fears around when it will occur, whether it will worsen, and how bad it will get. The psychological distress of period pain is associated with worsening depression, increased isolation, and worsened pain intensity.[5]

The more severe the pain, the greater the psychological distress. So how can parents help?

Adolescents depend heavily on the influences of family and friends. When they need medicine for period pain, they will most likely check their medicine cabinet at home. They are often confused about the differences in medication types and unsure about dosing.[6] Even if you've never considered using pain medication for period symptoms before, as their parent, you should have a basic understanding of which options are available and how to use them. Medicine utilization doesn't mean we forget about the usefulness of heat therapy, rest, dietary modifications, hydration, sleep, and other nonpharmacological interventions. It just means that we use every resource available to support the health and well-being of our children.

Parental support and response to period pain inform adolescent perceptions of their pain and their coping strategies. When parents normalize or dismiss pain, adolescents are less likely to get treatment. Untreated period pain is associated with higher rates of school absenteeism, reduced academic performance, decreased participation in social activities, and worsened well-being and quality of life. When parents acknowledge pain and show sympathy and support, adolescents have decreased psychological stress, improved emotional well-being, and improved quality of life. Parental support is especially critical for timely medical evaluation, access to prescribed medication, and adherence to hormonal therapy use.[7] By understanding period pain and recognizing when intervention is necessary, you can serve as a knowledgeable advocate for your child. Here's what you need to know.

Period pain, or the condition of having painful periods, is called dysmenorrhea. Although dysmenorrhea is often misunderstood to be limited to pelvic pain or cramps, it is associated with many symptoms. These symptoms include pain in the abdomen, pelvis, low back, and legs. It can also be associated with nausea, vomiting, and diarrhea. There are two main types of dysmenorrhea: primary and secondary. Primary dysmenorrhea is pain that is not associated with or felt to be due to an underlying condition. Secondary dysmenorrhea is due to an identifiable cause, like endometriosis, fibroids, a uterine anomaly, or an ovarian cyst.

Primary dysmenorrhea is the more common type and is due to the physiological release of prostaglandins from the uterine lining. Because prostaglandins are inflammatory chemicals, they cause a type of inflammatory response. Their release triggers contraction of the uterus and shedding of the uterine lining. Higher levels of prostaglandins are associated with higher levels of pain. The amount of prostaglandins peaks right before menstruation starts. This is why pain is typically worse just before your period or in the first one to two days of bleeding. In fact, the peak severity of most period pain is within twelve to sixteen hours of onset of bleeding. This predictable and self-limited characteristic of period cramps makes them ideal for self-guided treatment. Optimal management of primary dysmenorrhea is determined by the severity of the pain and the presence of associated symptoms.

There are many nonpharmacological ways to help manage period pain. Heat therapy is a common method. It is usually done by applying a heating pad or patch to the lower abdomen to relax the uterine muscles and increase blood flow. This helps to reduce the intensity of uterine contractions and promote significant and fairly rapid pain relief. While it is important to use pain therapy products as directed to avoid burns and thermal damage, heat therapy is safe and effective and can reasonably be used as an initial pain relief option.

Another nonpharmacological method that has been shown to improve period pain is physical exercise. Aerobic exercise for forty-five to sixty minutes at least three times per week is recommended. Low-intensity exercise like yoga and stretching also reduces menstrual pain. Other methods for period pain improvement include acupuncture, transcutaneous electrical nerve stimulation, and cognitive behavioral therapy. These methods can be used as initial therapy, alone or in combination with medications.

When period pain is unable to be tolerated or managed with the above options, pharmacological therapy is usually the next step. It is recommended to start with over-the-counter medications prior to using stronger prescription-strength options. Even so, it is appropriate to go ahead and start the process of medical evaluation in case stronger options become necessary.

The most effective medications available without a prescription are generally NSAIDs. These include ibuprofen and naproxen, which can be found in Aleve, Motrin, and Advil. These methods work well because they block the inflammatory effects of prostaglandins that are responsible for primary dysmenorrhea. Because there are some people who may have allergies, sensitivities, or contraindications to NSAID use, acetaminophen is a widely used alternative for period pain relief. Of note, acetaminophen is not as effective at treating period pain as NSAIDs are.

Combination pain medicines are commonly used by menstruators because of their multisymptom treatment. Most combination medicines contain acetaminophen in addition to other drugs that target common period-related symptoms like bloating and fatigue. Medications that include both acetaminophen (pain reliever) and pamabrom (diuretic) help manage pain as well as bloating. Other medications combine acetaminophen, pyrilamine maleate (antihistamine), and caffeine (diuretic) to manage fatigue, bloating, and pain like headaches, backaches, and cramps. Some medicines contain diuretics for bloating relief alone. Because they are available without a prescription, these medications are not just safe and effective, they are also accessible. If over-the-counter options don't achieve the desired level of relief, medical evaluation is the next step.

When looking for a medical provider to evaluate your adolescent's dysmenorrhea, you have many options. Many people start with their general practitioner or primary care provider. This can be their pediatrician, a family medicine physician, or an internal medicine doctor. The preferred provider for more complex dysmenorrhea management tends to be a gynecologist. A gynecologist is a physician who provides care for conditions that affect the female reproductive organs. A pediatric and adolescent gynecologist is one who is specially trained in the care of children and adolescents. It is my professional opinion that a gynecologist who has significant training and experience in caring for teens is the best option for evaluating an adolescent with dysmenorrhea. When you take your child in for evaluation, they may recommend diagnostic testing. This is how we distinguish between primary and secondary dysmenorrhea.

As previously mentioned, secondary dysmenorrhea is period pain due to an underlying cause. To identify that underlying cause, your medical provider may need to perform exams, tests, or even procedures. Once a diagnosis is made, treatment can be customized to that diagnosis and may include lifestyle modification, prescription pain medicine, a surgical procedure, or initiation of hormonal therapy. Even so, treatment does not have to be delayed until a diagnosis is made. If your child has been suffering with severe period pain, report it, and request medication to get them feeling some relief. It can take a few tries before finding the best pain management regimen that will work effectively for your child. It is important to be engaged, ask questions, report concerns, and follow up regularly in order to achieve the best outcome.

We may not be able to fix society's gender stereotypes and sex-based biases about pain, but we can support the menstruators in our lives with sympathy, kindness, awareness, and action. Period pain can be mild, and it can also be debilitating. Pain that prevents your child from doing their daily activities and causes them to wake up at night, miss school, sit out of sports, or withdraw from friends needs to be promptly evaluated. Pain that affects their body image, triggers anxiety, and causes depressive symptoms cannot be ignored. Period pain can affect every aspect of a menstruator's life. In this world that too often underestimates and dismisses menstrual symptoms, be diligent. Be informed. Be aware. Acknowledge and treat your child's pain.

12

Protect. Don't Police.

In 2019, U.S. rapper Clifford "T.I." Harris Jr. made the controversial claim during a podcast interview that he takes his teenage daughter to the gynecologist right after her birthday every year to check her hymen. He said these trips began after her sixteenth birthday, and his daughter was required to sign a waiver giving the doctor permission to tell him the results. He specifically said that he wanted to know if her hymen was "still intact." He went further to say that he clarifies with the doctor that she doesn't ride horses or bikes and doesn't play sports. At the time of the interview, his daughter was eighteen years old. When asked if he had the same standard for his fifteen-year-old son, he shared that he knew his son was sexually active and was fine with it.[1]

Although this story sounds like social media rage bait, it is real. And it represents a specific type of parent—one who willfully encourages double standards and shamelessly polices their child's sexual behaviors.

I take issue with T.I.'s behavior for a number of reasons. I'm angry that he spoke so publicly about his daughter's very personal information. I think it is beyond creepy for a father to discuss his daughter's hymen and to do so with countless strangers listening. It is also ignorant to believe that hymenal exams can determine virginity status. A simple Google search would have revealed this to be a myth. The doctor involved should never have agreed to perform the exam or disclose their findings. They are not practicing evidence-based medicine and could be putting their patients in danger by agreeing to do this type of "testing." I'm heartbroken for his daughter, who was not given an opportunity to truly consent to this, whether she signed a paper or not. Finally, I cannot stop wondering exactly what T.I. planned to do if he received results that he didn't like.

What he probably wanted to convey was that he was an involved father who took the protection of his daughter so seriously that he was informed on even the most intimate details. What he ended up conveying was his sexist and misinformed strategy for policing his daughter that had no protective potential at all.

If his daughter's hymen had not been intact and she had "failed" her virginity test, what would have been the next step? Because even if the hymen could accurately determine whether she'd had sex in the last year, the act would have already happened. As it would have related to the prior sexual encounters, the opportunity for true protection (providing education, preparation, or even contraception) would have come and gone. I suspect his response would have been disappointment, shame, and a punishment that he deemed appropriate for the crime. Policing.

The onset of puberty and periods brings on a myriad of new concerns related to everything from predators to sexuality and relationships. While many parents seek to protect their children from harm, they may end up policing them instead. Protecting and policing are not the same. The difference between the two terms is all about where one believes the true threat lies. When an issue occurs (and it will), your protection says, "I was right not to trust *them*," while your policing says, "I was right not to trust *you*." A parent protects because they believe there's a threat to their child. A parent polices because they believe their child is the threat.

If you want to protect your child, one of the first steps is engagement and open communication. Engagement with your child requires time, patience, curiosity, and understanding. You must set aside time to talk with them. This isn't just speaking as a family at dinnertime. It is not just sending a text here and there. It is intentional time for just the two of you to talk and share about life. Now it may seem as though getting an adolescent to open up and talk is nearly impossible, but you must try. You are the parent, so the burden is on you to make the connection. This is where patience comes in.

Adolescents rarely divulge information freely. They test you to see if you can be trusted first. Your child has been testing you for years, and you will have already taught them a lot about how they should expect you to respond. If you catastrophize small inconveniences or mistakes, they will hide these things from you to avoid drama. If you disclose their issues and concerns to others without their consent, they will censor their stories to protect their privacy. If you treat them differently when they share their most vulnerable and authentic truths, they will hide them to avoid shifting dynamics and causing awkwardness. If you haven't laid the best foundation for communication, you'll need patience and perseverance to reconnect.

Curiosity is one of the purest forms of love. When you love someone, you are genuinely curious about them. You want to know their perspective, their opinions, and their interests. You want to know what motivates them, what makes them sad, and what scares them. You want to know what they love, who they love, and how they love. You want to know how you can show up for them, how you can support their dreams, and how you can improve or correct mistakes that you may have made in the past. Be curious about your child and get to know who they truly are.

And when your curiosity is satisfied with answers and insight, they will need your understanding. They need to know that you love them no matter what. They need to know that you see them for who they are and not for what they did or didn't do. They need you to honor them as a unique and freethinking individual who has the right to live their life fully. Once you've established healthy communication, you must then use practical and proven methods for protection.

One area of concern in today's world that prior generations of parents didn't have to worry about is online safety. Because of the frequency with which we use digital media, our children can be influenced and accessed by more people than ever before. While there are many positive ways to use online platforms, many people use them for cyberbullying, grooming, and other inappropriate and harmful activities. Children and teens are especially vulnerable to these types of predators and require parental involvement to ensure their safety and protection.

Adolescents who perceive high levels of family support are less likely to engage in high-risk internet behaviors.[2] This means healthy and supportive parent-child relationships are inherently protective. As their parent, it is important that you monitor your child's daily internet use and set boundaries and restrictions as appropriate. Problematic internet use and online addiction are associated with higher risk of online victimization. Balancing internet rules and restrictions with trust and communication is more effective than restrictive parenting alone, and excessive restrictions may encourage your child to use the internet in secret. Be sure to provide them with relevant education on internet safety, acknowledge online risks, and maintain open communication about their online activities. It can be hard to keep up with technology and to protect from digital threats, but safety requires adjustment to change.

There are certain parental fears that will likely never change. The fear of early sexual activity or premature sexual debut is one that's been around for ages. For many parents, cultures, and communities, puberty is a coming of age that inevitably ushers in sexual exploration, disobedience, dishonesty, and disrespect. This is such a strong association that parental attitudes can harden at the first sign of pubertal change.

Sexual awareness, sexual exploration, and increased interest in romantic relationships are associated with pubertal development. As kids' bodies change in puberty, their emotions, motivations, and interests change as well. This is normal and must be treated as such. When adolescents are punished for normal physiological changes, they cannot win. Instead of shaming children for growing into young adults, we should be equipping them to make the transition with wisdom, safety, and agency.

Supportive parent relationships and open communication about sexual health can positively impact adolescents' sexual emotions and autonomy. Higher quality parent-child relationships are associated with higher adolescent self-esteem. Self-esteem plays a huge role in sexual behaviors, risk-taking, and decision-making. On the other hand, low adolescent self-esteem is associated with earlier sexual initiation, higher likelihood for unprotected sexual encounters, and engagement with multiple sexual partners.[3] Investing in your child with time, affirming language, and encouragement teaches them self-worth and builds their self-esteem. Self-esteem is protective.

Unfortunately, many parents try to control their children with fear. Scare tactics, like exaggerated threats that emphasize punishment and shame, are not effective and can lead to negative psychological outcomes. This makes sense because fear causes psychological distress. Adolescents who instead receive factual information about sexual health are better prepared to handle the changes of puberty and navigate their increased sexual awareness.

Sexual and Gender Identity

An important aspect of this growing sexual awareness is sexual and gender identity. Sexual and gender minority youth are especially impacted by parental influence during pubertal development. The majority of adolescents develop their sexual identity as a continuous process. Through sexual attractions and experiences, they form preferences and attitudes. As they begin to better establish their personal identity, sexual and gender minority youth are constantly made to face the sexual and gender expectations of a heteronormative society. Ultimately, they must come to terms with an identity that is inconsistent with what is expected of them. This is described as one of the most stressful times for many sexual and gender minority adolescents.

As if the stressors of puberty weren't enough, many younger teenagers deal with the additional stress of revealing their sexual or gender identity. It has been well documented that the average age of coming out has dropped from twenty years old in the 1970s to fourteen years old in the 2000s. For sexual and gender minority adolescents, the decision to share one's identity makes them vulnerable to rejection and abandonment. While in the United States, many children experience warmth and acceptance from their parents when they disclose their sexual and gender identities, others experience maltreatment or even hostility that can be traumatic and isolating.

Coming out during the pubertal years is associated with increased experiences of homophobia as well as negative peer behaviors and increased victimization. Family acceptance, especially parental acceptance, can serve as a buffer from negative societal effects outside the home. Parental support is critical for all adolescents but especially sexual and gender minorities. It is critical for health, well-being, and adjustment. In fact, in many cases, it can be the difference between life and death.[4]

Adolescence is a period of emerging identity development with a growing need for increased independence. While the multitude of emotional, physical, and social changes requires parental support, the development of agency and autonomy requires measured freedom. A child who feels policed by their parents will feel suffocated by unrealistic expectations, unrelenting surveillance, and undeserved harassment. A child who feels protected by their parents will have the security necessary for self-discovery, safe exploration, and healthy social connections. It is impossible to understate the importance of your role as a parent during adolescence. The dynamic nature of your role mirrors the dynamic changes in your child. So give them space, but stay close. You never know when they will need you next.

13

Trust Them

I've always loved the water. As a child, my favorite summer activity was to go to the local pool to swim. I loved the refreshing and weightless feeling of being in the pool. I loved blowing bubbles and hearing the distorted sound of my own voice while under the water. I loved the way tiny water beads would form and sit on top of my curly hair and roll down onto my eyelashes. The splashing, laughter, and fun filled my little heart with joy. But my joy was abruptly interrupted one day when my older brother and sister began to prefer to swim in the deep end of the pool. I wasn't allowed to swim there due to my age-related lack of height and experience. So I began to watch with building resentment as they jumped off the diving board, performed flips, and played games. I did everything in my power to send them scathing looks as I moped around the area marked "three feet and under" in my arm floaties.

With the help of time and swimming lessons, I got taller and better at swimming. My dad noticed my efforts to improve and volunteered to work with me. He maintained that I had to be able to swim a decent distance without getting tired or needing to come up for air in order to swim in the deep end. To help me meet these criteria, he would carry me out to four feet and tell me to hold on to the side of the pool, and he'd head toward the other side. He would then ask me to swim to him.

If I looked up and didn't like how far he was standing, I'd shake my head and ask him to come closer. He would reluctantly comply, knowing that I wouldn't even push off the wall until I felt like he was close enough to ensure success. On my first try, I made it to him, but barely. I assumed I'd underestimated the distance and quickly asked to try again. After the second and third attempts, I began to get suspicious. Something was definitely off. By the fourth and fifth time, I had him figured out. He was agreeing to stand where I asked him to, but once I began swimming, he was moving. It was almost undetectable, because he'd wait until I was just about to reach him to slowly step back. He'd do this until I looked like I was getting tired or about to quit and would then scoop me up out of the water. When I asked why he did this, he said it was because I never would have found out what I was capable of otherwise. Meaning if he'd stayed where I asked and stepped in to "save" me too soon, I wouldn't have learned how far I could swim on my own. I still think of his unorthodox method whenever I swim laps in a pool.

Puberty is a time of increased awareness, comparison, and

change. As bodies develop, new interests emerge, and relationships shift. There is a growing desire for increased independence as well as a gradual necessity for greater responsibility. Because this transition is ultimately occurring as a part of the journey to adulthood, we must accept that the roles we once played in our children's lives have to change.

We must be careful not to overparent. Overparenting is characterized by developmentally inappropriate and excessive involvement. The "developmentally inappropriate" distinction is key. It is not to say that the supervision, correction, and support that you offer are inherently inappropriate. It means that they are not appropriate for this new stage of development. What could have been considered as normal parenting for your child four years ago can be overparenting for your child today.

Understanding the concept of overparenting is important because overly controlling parenting is associated with several negative psychological effects on adolescents. It is linked to increased levels of depression and anxiety. It triggers frustration of adolescents' basic psychological needs, restricting their ability to access and develop emotion regulation strategies. Overparenting also negatively affects self-esteem and self-efficacy. Self-efficacy is defined as a person's belief in their ability to do something, like successfully complete a task or reach a goal. Because of this impact, overparenting is shown to be negatively related to leader emergence, meaning overparented adolescents may be less likely to become leaders later in life.[1]

Most parents who are excessively involved in their children's lives have good intentions. They are often trying to protect their children by shielding them from disappointment, inconvenience, and adversity. Unfortunately, when adolescents never experience challenges, they fail to develop their problem-solving and decision-making skills. This further limits their ability to learn coping strategies and increases the likelihood that they will experience anxiety when they inevitably face challenges on their own. The long-term effects of overparenting can be significant, including social disconnection, increased substance use, and increased depression and anxiety in adulthood.[2] To avoid the numerous negative effects of overparenting, we must employ strategies that are proven to promote adolescent independence and well-being.

Open and honest communication along with warmth and support are continued themes in healthy adolescent parenting. While some parents may feel tempted to increase strictness and harshness during the adolescent years, it is clear that a supportive environment is the best place for an adolescent to explore, make mistakes, and learn.[3]

Balanced involvement is also critical. It is important to avoid micromanaging but also remain a reliable and present resource when needed. For example, instead of packing period products for your adolescent to take to school, instead ask them to talk through what they need for the day. As they list off their homework, their musical instrument, and their athletic uniform, see if they will remember their period products without you reminding them. If they don't, give them a gentle nudge by asking if they're on their period. Allow them to conclude that failure to pack period products might result in an accident or stain on their clothes. By connecting their actions to potential consequences, they can strengthen their planning skills, ultimately motivated by the outcomes they desire.

It is also important to encourage problem-solving skills by allowing your child to face challenges and come up with their own solutions. If they forget their homework, instead of bringing it directly to their school, have them work out a plan to submit the assignment at a later time or make up the work in another way. If they have a social conflict, lend a listening ear as they work through options for resolution. Ensure that they consider their personal values and reach a decision that doesn't compromise their standards.[4]

Promote healthy habits by being a good example. Demonstrate what healthy eating, proper physical activity, adequate sleep, and appropriate online and screen usage looks like. Expecting your adolescent to have better health routines than you have ever had is unreasonable. Instead of increasing supervision and dictating the specifics of their nutrition, exercise routines, and leisure time, model the balance and health you want them to have.

Set clear boundaries. Consider your family values, standards for safety, and guiding principles. Set family and household rules that support these values along with consequences for when the rules are broken. This can help your child understand their role in the family, their responsibilities in the home, and the expectations you have of them. Finally, you must trust them.

Trust is a decision. You must decide to give your child the opportunity to show you that they are responsible, mature, and reliable. The opportunities don't have to be extreme, but they do have to exist. When you provide them with opportunities to exercise their autonomy, be prepared for the possibility that they will make different decisions than you might make. As long as they are healthy, happy, respectful, honest, and safe, make an effort to show your support and honor their growing power. Understand that there are multiple ways to show up well in life, and your child deserves to chart their own path.

Remember that you know your child better than anyone, and it is your responsibility and privilege to prepare them for a life where they are healthy and whole. Where society and modern culture may fail them, you can offer gentle correction, sincere understanding, and unconditional love. If you have employed the lessons of this book, you should have been able to provide your child with shame-free support, medically accurate information, and age-appropriate guidance. Now it is time to trust in the process and enjoy watching them grow.

Much like my father did with me, take gentle steps back until they realize the fullness of their potential. Encourage them to push themselves and to always believe they can achieve more. And when they grow weary or need your help, let them know you're always there. As a parent, you're never done or no longer needed. The way you are needed just changes.

Afterword

Every revolution starts with a personal desire for change, beginning with a smoldering ember of hope that grows into a burning imperative for better. That's how this book began for me.

I entered pediatric and adolescent gynecology because I genuinely wanted to change the early reproductive health experiences of young people. I wanted them to see a doctor who saw them not as problems to fix but as people to support, heal, and empower. I developed my practice style with that in mind. The culture of my practice was centered around creating a safe space that was inclusive, free of judgment, and free of shame. This allowed me to build rapport, grow trust, and foster relationships with both my patients and their parents. I was able to see different parenting styles at work, take note of the manifestations of misinformation, and combat the unintended consequences of pain. While I've never taken for granted the remarkable privilege it is to be able to listen to and learn about the lives and experiences of others, I didn't always understand how rare and valuable that perspective was.

Their openness gave me the insight necessary to appreciate the strengths of my work as well as its inherent limitations. I was just one person that my patients saw a few times a year for a few moments in their lives. I couldn't fully overcome the influences of social media, heal their traumas of the past, or reconcile the inconsistencies of religion or the injustices of society. My small efforts positively impacted many, but there were so many more that I would never reach.

As I attempted to spread more awareness, I noted daunting and unnerving political and social shifts in the world around me. Respected community organizations, schools, and even books were being attacked for providing critical information on reproductive health. Laws were being passed that forbid instruction on menstrual health and criminalized the provision of resources and education. I'd sparked a tiny movement, but this called for large-scale change.

I needed to reach those who understood that reproductive health awareness and autonomy were foundational to self-fulfillment and liberation. I needed to reach those who didn't seek to reduce children to gender-based social constructs and expectations but instead sought to enhance and enrich children's lives with boundless possibilities. I needed to reach those who wanted children to not just exist but thrive. It was through the identification of this need that I came to realize the power of parents. There is no better partner, ally, or collaborator in the work of saving the future than parents.

So I compiled the stories, lessons, and histories that shape our beliefs and attitudes around reproductive health. I gathered the studies from leading journals and the medically accurate anatomy and physiology from years of medical practice and training. I took what I have learned, witnessed, and lived and put it in this book so that you might combine it with your inherent power and influence.

It is my hope that the words on these pages will allow you to feel better prepared for what's to come. That you might do the work to unlearn, forgive, and heal so your child can experience puberty with the confidence, support, and safety that many of us weren't able to have.

It is my prayer that you begin to see your growing adolescent as an individual with inherent value and divine purpose. I hope you begin to view this time as a coming of age instead of a coming of trials. I hope boldness overcomes uncertainty and facts replace fears. I hope you trade harshness for warmth and trauma for transformation.

The true revolution is in the changing of beliefs, the enlightening of minds, and the unburdening of childhoods.

In a world that is restricting education, defunding health research, erasing diversity, and villainizing authentic expression, the customized and unique application of information to fit your child's needs is revolutionary. It is up to parents to take on the charge of protecting the reproductive freedoms and futures of our children. When we rewrite the rules, we reclaim our power, a power we've always had but haven't always wielded. The choice is yours. The time is now. Let's start a revolution.

Notes

Chapter 1: Opting Out Is Not an Option

1. "History of Sex Education in the U.S.," Planned Parenthood, February 9, 2017, https://www.plannedparenthood.org/uploads/filer_public/da/67/da67fd5d-631d-438a-85e8-a446d90fd1e3/20170209_sexed_d04_1.pdf.
2. Eric A. DeGroff, "Sex Education in the Public Schools and the Accommodation of Familial Rights," *Children's Legal Rights Journal* 26 (2006): 21, https://ssrn.com/abstract=1985251; Hopkins v. Hamden Board of Education, 29 Conn. Supp. 397, 289 A.2d 914 (1971), https://case-law.vlex.com/vid/hopkins-v-hamden-bd-890417521.
3. T. W. Smith and J. Son, *General Social Survey 2012 Final Report: Trends in Public Attitudes About Sexual Morality* (NORC at the University of Chicago, 2013), https://www.norc.org/content/dam/norc-org/pdfs/Trends%20in%20Sexual%20Moraility_Final.pdf.
4. Marla Eisenberg et al., "Increased Parent Support for Comprehensive Sexuality Education Over 15 Years," *Journal of Adolescent Health* 71, no. 6 (December 2022): 744–50, https://doi.org/10.1016/j.jadohealth.2022.08.005.
5. Leigh E. Szucs et al., "Overwhelming Support for Sexual Health Education in U.S. Schools: A Meta-Analysis of 23 Surveys Conducted Between 2000 and 2016," *Journal of Adolescent Health* 70, no. 4 (April 2022): 598–606, https://doi.org/10.1016/j.jadohealth.2021.05.016.
6. Jeffrey L. Hurst et al., "Parents' Attitudes Towards the Content of Sex Education in the USA: Associations with Religiosity and Political Orientation," *Sex Education* 24, no. 1 (January 2024): 108–24, https://doi.org/10.1080/14681811.2022.2162871.
7. "Evidence-Based Sex Education: The Case for Sustained Federal Support," Guttmacher Institute, April 2025, https://www.guttmacher.org/fact-sheet/sex-education.
8. Laura D. Lindberg et al., "Adolescents' Receipt of Sex Education in a Nationally

Representative Sample, 2011–2019," *Journal of Adolescent Health* 70, no. 2 (February 2022): 290–97, https://doi.org/10.1016/j.jadohealth.2021.08.027.

9. Jaclyn Diaz, "Florida's Governor Signs Controversial Law Opponents Dubbed 'Don't Say Gay,'" NPR, March 28, 2022, https://www.npr.org/2022/03/28/1089221657/dont-say-gay-florida-desantis.
10. Lauren Brensel, "Pause the Period: State Bill Would Ban Mention of Menstruation in Elementary Schools," *Independent Florida Alligator*, March 27, 2023, https://www.alligator.org/article/2023/03/pause-the-period-state-bill-would-ban-mention-of-menstruation-in-elementary-schools.
11. Erin Digitale, "Age That Kids Acquire Mobile Phones Not Linked to Well-Being, Says Stanford Medicine Study," Stanford Medicine News Center, November 21, 2022, https://med.stanford.edu/news/all-news/2022/11/children-mobile-phone-age.html.
12. Common Sense Media, *Teens and Pornography: A New Research Report from Common Sense*, March 2022, https://www.commonsensemedia.org/sites/default/files/research/report/2022-teens-and-pornography-final-web.pdf.
13. Grace B. Jhe et al., "Pornography Use Among Adolescents and the Role of Primary Care," *Family Medicine and Community Health* 11, no. 1 (January 2023): e001776, https://doi.org/10.1136/fmch-2022-001776.
14. "State of the Period 2023," Period.org, 2023, https://period.org/uploads/2023-State-of-the-Period-Study.pdf.
15. Devendra Raj Singh et al., "Parental Knowledge and Communication with Their Adolescent on Sexual and Reproductive Health Issues in Nepal," *PLOS One* 18, no. 7 (July 2023): e0289116, https://doi.org/10.1371/journal.pone.0289116.
16. Elizabeth Aku Baku et al., "Effects of Parents Training on Parents' Knowledge and Attitudes About Adolescent Sexuality in Accra Metropolis, Ghana," *Reproductive Health* 14 (2017): 101, https://doi.org/10.1186/s12978-017-0363-9.

Chapter 3: Unlearn the Negativity

1. Trisha Maharaj and Inga T. Winkler, "Transnational Engagements: Cultural and Religious Practices Related to Menstruation," in *The Palgrave Handbook of Critical Menstruation Studies*, ed. Chris Bobel et al. (Palgrave Macmillan, 2020), 163–74, https://doi.org/10.1007/978-981-15-0614-7_15.
2. Hong Ju et al., "The Prevalence and Risk Factors of Dysmenorrhea," *Epidemiologic Reviews* 36, no. 1 (2014): 104–13, https://doi.org/10.1093/epirev/mxt009.
3. Ranit Mishori et al., "The Little Tissue That Couldn't: Dispelling Myths About the Hymen's Role in Determining Sexual History and Assault," *Reproductive Health* 16, no. 1 (June 3, 2019): 74, https://doi.org/10.1186/s12978-019-0731-8.
4. Jingyi Tang et al., "Diet and Nutrients Intakes During Infancy and Childhood in

Relation to Early Puberty: A Systematic Review and Meta-Analysis," *Nutrients* 14, no. 23 (2022): 5004, https://doi.org/10.3390/nu14235004.

5. Mishori et al., "Little Tissue That Couldn't," 74.
6. "Comprehensive Sexuality Education," World Health Organization, May 18, 2023, https://www.who.int/news-room/questions-and-answers/item/comprehensive-sexuality-education.
7. Alexandra Morales et al., "Sexually Unexperienced Adolescents Benefit the Most from a Sexual Education Program for Adolescents: A Longitudinal Cluster Randomized Controlled Study," *AIDS Education and Prevention* 32, no. 6 (December 2020): 493–511, https://doi.org/10.1521/aeap.2020.32.6.493.
8. Jacqueline A. Noonan, "A History of Pediatric Specialties: The Development of Pediatric Cardiology," *Pediatric Research* 56, no. 2 (August 2004): 298–306, https://doi.org/10.1203/01.PDR.0000132662.73362.96.

Chapter 4: Body Basics: A Simple Explanation of Your Child's Anatomy and Why It Is Important for Both of You to Understand It

1. Dina El-Hamamsy et al., "Public Understanding of Female Genital Anatomy and Pelvic Organ Prolapse (POP): A Questionnaire-Based Pilot Study," *International Urogynecology Journal* 33, no. 2 (February 2022): 309–18, https://doi.org/10.1007/s00192-021-04727-9.
2. Radhika Patnam et al., "Defining Normal Apical Vaginal Support: A Relook at the POSST Study," *International Urogynecology Journal* 30 (2019): 45–51, https://doi.org/10.1007/s00192-018-3681-8.

Chapter 5: Everyday Essentials: Understanding Vulvovaginal Health and Period Product Safety

1. Omar M. Shaaban et al., "Vaginal Douching by Women with Vulvovaginitis and Relation to Reproductive Health Hazards," *BMC Women's Health* 13 (May 14, 2013): 23, https://doi.org/10.1186/1472-6874-13-23; Barbara Hansen Cottrell, "Vaginal Douching," *Journal of Obstetric, Gynecologic & Neonatal Nursing* 32, no. 1 (January–February 2003): 12–18, https://doi.org/10.1177/0884217502239796.
2. Alice S. Weissfeld, "The History of Tampons: From Ancient Times to an FDA-Regulated Medical Device," *Clinical Microbiology Newsletter* 32, no. 10 (May 2010): 73–76, https://doi.org/10.1016/j.clinmicnews.2010.04.003.
3. Karan Babbar and Supriya Garikipati, "What Socio-Demographic Factors Support Disposable vs. Sustainable Menstrual Choices? Evidence from India's National Family Health Survey-5," *PLOS One* 18, no. 8 (August 17, 2023): e0290350, https://doi.org/10.1371/journal.pone.0290350.

4. Laura Medina-Perucha et al., "Use and Perceptions on Reusable and Non-Reusable Menstrual Products in Spain: A Mixed-Methods Study," *PLOS One* 17, no. 3 (March 17, 2022): e0265646, https://doi.org/10.1371/journal.pone.0265646.
5. Jenni A. Shearston et al., "Tampons as a Source of Exposure to Metal(loid)s," *Environment International* 190 (August 2024): 108849, https://doi.org/10.1016/j.envint.2024.108849; Joanna Marroquin et al., "Chemicals in Menstrual Products: A Systematic Review," *BJOG: An International Journal of Obstetrics and Gynaecology* 131, no. 5 (April 2024): 655–64, https://doi.org/10.1111/1471-0528.17668.
6. Mehruba Anwar Parris et al., "ACMT Position Statement: No Evidence That Tampons Cause Metal Poisoning," American College of Medical Toxicology, October 2, 2024, https://www.acmt.net/news/acmt-position-statement-no-evidence-that-tampons-cause-metal-poisoning/.
7. Centers for Disease Control and Prevention, "Epidemiological Notes and Reports Toxic-Shock Syndrome, United States, 1970–1982," *Morbidity and Mortality Weekly Report* 31, no. 16 (April 30, 1982): 201–4, https://www.cdc.gov/mmwr/preview/mmwrhtml/00000248.htm.
8. "Healthy Habits: Menstrual Hygiene," Centers for Disease Control and Prevention, May 7, 2024, https://www.cdc.gov/hygiene/about/menstrual-hygiene.html.
9. Sharra L. Vostral, "Rely and Toxic Shock Syndrome: A Technological Health Crisis," *Yale Journal of Biology and Medicine* 84, no. 4 (December 2011): 447–59, https://www.ncbi.nlm.nih.gov/pmc/articles/PMC3238331/.

Chapter 6: Prepare for Puberty: What to Expect to Happen When So You're Not Caught by Surprise

1. Bo Yang et al., "Maternal Age at Menarche and Pubertal Timing in Boys and Girls: A Cohort Study from Chongqing, China," *Journal of Adolescent Health* 68, no. 3 (March 2021): 508–16, https://doi.org/10.1016/j.jadohealth.2020.06.036; S. Sørensen et al., "Maternal Age at Menarche and Pubertal Development in Sons and Daughters: A Nationwide Cohort Study," *Human Reproduction* 33, no. 11 (November 2018): 2043–50, https://doi.org/10.1093/humrep/dey287.
2. Mary S. Wolff et al., "Environmental Exposures and Puberty in Inner-City Girls," *Environmental Research* 107, no. 3 (July 2008): 393–400, https://doi.org/10.1016/j.envres.2008.03.006.
3. Mickey Emmanuel and Brooke R. Bokor, "Tanner Stages," in *StatPearls* (StatPearls Publishing, January 2025–), https://www.ncbi.nlm.nih.gov/books/NBK470280/.
4. Amy E. Lacroix et al., "Physiology, Menarche," in *StatPearls* (StatPearls Publishing, January 2025–), https://www.ncbi.nlm.nih.gov/books/NBK470216/.

5. Jason Rafferty, "Gender Identity Development in Children," HealthyChildren.org, last updated May 7, 2024, https://www.healthychildren.org/English/ages-stages/gradeschool/Pages/Gender-Identity-and-Gender-Confusion-In-Children.aspx.
6. Vishna Shah et al., "Effect of a Multicomponent Intervention to Improve Menstrual Health and Hygiene and School Attendance Among Adolescent Girls in the Gambia (MEGAMBO Trial)," *Journal of Adolescent Health* 76, no. 5 (May 2025): 879–88, https://doi.org/10.1016/j.jadohealth.2024.12.018.
7. Rebecca Lane Evans et al., "Systematic Review of Educational Interventions to Improve the Menstrual Health of Young Adolescent Girls," *BMJ Open* 12, no. 6 (June 8, 2022): e057204, https://doi.org/10.1136/bmjopen-2021–057204.
8. Julia L. Shenkman et al., "Building Menstrual Health and Hygiene-Supportive Environments: Exploring Teachers' Experience in Rural Western Kenya," *Frontiers in Public Health* 11 (July 25, 2023): 1206069, https://doi.org/10.3389/fpubh.2023.1206069.
9. Mahbub-Ul Alam et al., "Evaluation of a Menstrual Hygiene Intervention in Urban and Rural Schools in Bangladesh: A Pilot Study," *BMC Public Health* 22, no. 1 (June 2, 2022): 1100, https://doi.org/10.1186/s12889-022-13478-1.
10. Bikis Yaynie Shibeshi et al., "Disparities in Menstrual Hygiene Management Between Urban and Rural Schoolgirls in Northeast, Ethiopia," *PLOS One* 16, no. 9 (September 30, 2021): e0257853, https://doi.org/10.1371/journal.pone.0257853.
11. Burcu Kardaş et al., "Early Puberty Paradox: An Investigation of Anxiety Levels of Mothers and Children, Children's Quality of Life, and Psychiatric Diagnoses," *European Journal of Pediatrics* 182, no. 8 (August 2023): 3775–83, https://doi.org/10.1007/s00431-023-05057-2.
12. Margaret L. Schmitt et al., "'It Always Gets Pushed Aside': Qualitative Perspectives on Puberty and Menstruation Education in U.S.A. Schools," *Frontiers in Reproductive Health* 4 (October 21, 2022): 1018217, https://doi.org/10.3389/frph.2022.1018217.

Chapter 7: How to Show Up in All the Right Ways: Supporting Your Child Unconditionally During Puberty and Their First Period

1. Julianna Deardorff et al., "Pubertal Timing and Mexican-Origin Girls' Internalizing and Externalizing Symptoms: The Influence of Harsh Parenting," *Developmental Psychology* 49, no. 9 (September 2013): 1790–804, https://doi.org/10.1037/a0031016.
2. Rebecca M. B. White et al., "Contextual Amplification or Attenuation of Pubertal Timing Effects on Depressive Symptoms Among Mexican American Girls," *Journal of Adolescent Health* 50, no. 6 (June 2012): 565–71, https://doi.org/10.1016/j.jadohealth.2011.10.006.

3. Bamidele M. Bello et al., "Adolescent and Parental Reactions to Puberty in Nigeria and Kenya: A Cross-Cultural and Intergenerational Comparison," *Journal of Adolescent Health* 61, no. 4S (2017): S35–S41, https://doi.org/10.1016/j.jadohealth.2017.03.014.
4. Sanne P. A. Rasing et al., "The Association Between Perceived Maternal and Paternal Psychopathology and Depression and Anxiety Symptoms in Adolescent Girls," *Frontiers in Psychology* 6 (July 21, 2015): 963, https://doi.org/10.3389/fpsyg.2015.00963.
5. Yulia E. Chentsova Dutton et al., "Perceived Parental Support and Adolescents' Positive Self-Beliefs and Levels of Distress Across Four Countries," *Frontiers in Psychology* 11 (March 3, 2020): 353, https://doi.org/10.3389/fpsyg.2020.00353.
6. Shu-Sha Angie Guan et al., "Parental Support Buffers the Association of Depressive Symptoms with Cortisol and C-Reactive Protein During Adolescence," *Brain, Behavior, and Immunity* 57 (October 2016): 134–43, https://doi.org/10.1016/j.bbi.2016.03.007.

Chapter 8: Teaching the Things You Had to Learn the Hard Way: Showing Your Child How to Live in the World as a Menstruator

1. Altangarvdi Borjigen et al., "Status and Factors of Menstrual Knowledge, Attitudes, Behaviors and Their Correlation with Psychological Stress in Adolescent Girls," *Journal of Pediatric and Adolescent Gynecology* 32, no. 6 (December 2019): 584–89, https://doi.org/10.1016/j.jpag.2019.08.007.
2. Emma L. Ratliff et al., "Supportive Parent-Adolescent Relationships as a Foundation for Adolescent Emotion Regulation and Adjustment," *Frontiers in Psychology* 14 (2023): 1193449, https://doi.org/10.3389/fpsyg.2023.1193449.
3. Jennifer L. Bercaw-Pratt et al., "The Incidence, Attitudes and Practices of the Removal of Pubic Hair as a Body Modification," *Journal of Pediatric and Adolescent Gynecology* 25, no. 1 (February 2012): 12–14, https://doi.org/10.1016/j.jpag.2011.06.015.
4. Rachel V. Reynolds et al., "Guidelines of Care for the Management of Acne Vulgaris," *Journal of the American Academy of Dermatology* 90, no. 5 (2024): 1006.e1–1006.e30, https://doi.org/10.1016/j.jaad.2023.12.017.

Chapter 9: More Than Birth Control: Understanding the Role of Hormones as Medicine

1. Geri D. Hewitt and Jennie Yoost, "Gynecologic Management of Adolescents and Young Women with Seizure Disorders: ACOG Committee Opinion No. 806," *Obstetrics & Gynecology* 135, no. 5 (May 2020): e213–20, https://doi.org/10.1097/AOG.0000000000003827.

2. Leslie Skeith and Shannon M. Bates, "Estrogen, Progestin, and Beyond: Thrombotic Risk and Contraceptive Choices," *Hematology: American Society of Hematology Education Program* 2024, no. 1 (December 6, 2024): 644–51, https://doi.org/10.1182/hematology.2024000591.

Chapter 11: Acknowledge and Treat Pain

1. Mika Guzikevits et al., "Sex Bias in Pain Management Decisions," *Proceedings of the National Academy of Sciences of the United States of America* 121, no. 33 (August 13, 2024): e2401331121, https://doi.org/10.1073/pnas.2401331121.
2. Lanlan Zhang et al., "Gender Biases in Estimation of Others' Pain," *Journal of Pain* 22, no. 9 (September 2021): 1048–59, https://doi.org/10.1016/j.jpain.2021.03.001.
3. Katherine Allyn et al., "'Tomorrow, I'll Be Fine': Impacts and Coping Mechanisms in Adolescents and Young Adults with Primary Dysmenorrhoea," *Journal of Advanced Nursing* 76, no. 10 (August 5, 2020): 2637–47, https://doi.org/10.1111/jan.14460.
4. Afsane Bahrami et al., "Neuropsychological Function in Relation to Dysmenorrhea in Adolescents," *European Journal of Obstetrics & Gynecology and Reproductive Biology* 215 (August 2017): 224–29, https://doi.org/10.1016/j.ejogrb.2017.06.030.
5. Nilfer Sahin et al., "Assessment of Anxiety-Depression Levels and Perceptions of Quality of Life in Adolescents with Dysmenorrhea," *Reproductive Health* 15, no. 1 (January 26, 2018): 13, https://doi.org/10.1186/s12978-018-0453-3.
6. Mike Armour et al., "Self-Care Strategies and Sources of Knowledge on Menstruation in 12,526 Young Women with Dysmenorrhea: A Systematic Review and Meta-Analysis," *PLOS One* 14, no. 7 (July 24, 2019): e0220103, https://doi.org/10.1371/journal.pone.0220103.
7. Geri D. Hewitt and Karen R. Gerancher, "Dysmenorrhea and Endometriosis in the Adolescent: ACOG Committee Opinion No. 760," *Obstetrics & Gynecology* 132, no. 6 (December 2018): e249–58, https://doi.org/10.1097/AOG.0000000000002978.

Chapter 12: Protect. Don't Police.

1. E. J. Dickson, "It Isn't Just T.I.—Virginity Testing Is a Worldwide Problem," *Rolling Stone*, November 6, 2019, https://www.rollingstone.com/culture/culture-news/ti-gynecologist-virginity-test-908990/.
2. Juwon Hwang and Catalina L. Toma, "The Role of Mental Well-Being and Perceived Parental Supportiveness in Adolescents' Problematic Internet Use: Moderation Analysis," *JMIR Mental Health* 8, no. 9 (September 2021): e26203, https://doi.org/10.2196/26203.

3. Renske Keizer et al., "Perceived Quality of the Mother-Adolescent and Father-Adolescent Attachment Relationship and Adolescents' Self-Esteem," *Journal of Youth and Adolescence* 48, no. 6 (2019): 1203–17, https://doi.org/10.1007/s10964-019-01007-0.
4. W. Roger Mills-Koonce et al., "The Significance of Parenting and Parent-Child Relationships for Sexual and Gender Minority Adolescents," *Journal of Research on Adolescence* 28, no. 3 (September 2018): 637–49, https://doi.org/10.1111/jora.12404.

Chapter 13: Trust Them

1. Majid Sadoughi, "Overparenting and Adolescent's Trait Anxiety: Unraveling the Roles of Basic Psychological Needs Frustration and Emotion Dysregulation," *Acta Psychologica* 251 (November 2024): 104579, https://doi.org/10.1016/j.actpsy.2024.104579.
2. Qi Zhang and Wongeun Ji, "Overparenting and Offspring Depression, Anxiety, and Internalizing Symptoms: A Meta-Analysis," *Development and Psychopathology* 36, no. 3 (2024): 1307–22, https://doi.org/10.1017/s095457942300055x.
3. Anne Bülow et al., "Universal Ingredients to Parenting Teens: Parental Warmth and Autonomy Support Promote Adolescent Well-Being in Most Families," *Scientific Reports* 12 (October 7, 2022): 16836, https://doi.org/10.1038/s41598-022-21071-0.
4. Marie B. H. Yap et al., "Parenting Strategies for Reducing the Risk of Adolescent Depression and Anxiety Disorders: A Delphi Consensus Study," *Journal of Affective Disorders* 156 (March 2014): 67–75, https://doi.org/10.1016/j.jad.2013.11.017.

Bibliography

Alam, Mahbub-Ul, Farhana Sultana, Erin C. Hunter, et al. "Evaluation of a Menstrual Hygiene Intervention in Urban and Rural Schools in Bangladesh: A Pilot Study." *BMC Public Health* 22, no. 1 (June 2, 2022): 1100. https://doi.org/10.1186/s12889-022-13478-1.

Allyn, Katherine, Subhadra Evans, Laura C. Seidman, and Laura A. Payne. "'Tomorrow, I'll Be Fine': Impacts and Coping Mechanisms in Adolescents and Young Adults with Primary Dysmenorrhoea." *Journal of Advanced Nursing* 76, no. 10 (August 5, 2020): 2637–47. https://doi.org/10.1111/jan.14460.

Armour, Mike, Kelly Parry, Mahmoud A. Al-Dabbas, et al. "Self-Care Strategies and Sources of Knowledge on Menstruation in 12,526 Young Women with Dysmenorrhea: A Systematic Review and Meta-Analysis." *PLOS One* 14, no. 7 (July 24, 2019): e0220103. https://doi.org/10.1371/journal.pone.0220103.

Babbar, Karan, and Supriya Garikipati. "What Socio-Demographic Factors Support Disposable vs. Sustainable Menstrual Choices? Evidence from India's National Family Health Survey-5." *PLOS One* 18, no. 8 (August 17, 2023): e0290350. https://doi.org/10.1371/journal.pone.0290350.

Bahrami, Afsane, Hamidreza Sadeghnia, Amir Avan, et al. "Neuropsychological Function in Relation to Dysmenorrhea in Adolescents." *European Journal of Obstetrics & Gynecology and Reproductive Biology* 215 (August 2017): 224–29. https://doi.org/10.1016/j.ejogrb.2017.06.030.

Baku, Elizabeth Aku, Isaac Agbemafle, and Richard M. K. Adanu. "Effects of Parents Training on Parents' Knowledge and Attitudes About Adolescent Sexuality in Accra Metropolis, Ghana." *Reproductive Health* 14 (2017): 101. https://doi.org/10.1186/s12978-017-0363-9.

Bello, Bamidele M., Adesegun O. Fatusi, Oluwatomi E. Adepoju, et al. "Adolescent and Parental Reactions to Puberty in Nigeria and Kenya: A Cross-Cultural and Intergenerational Comparison." *Journal of Adolescent Health* 61, no. 4S (2017): S35–S41. https://doi.org/10.1016/j.jadohealth.2017.03.014.

Bercaw-Pratt, Jennifer L., Xiomara M. Santos, Judith Sanchez, Leslie Ayensu-Coker, Denise R. Nebgen, and Jennifer E. Dietrich. "The Incidence, Attitudes and

Practices of the Removal of Pubic Hair as a Body Modification." *Journal of Pediatric and Adolescent Gynecology* 25, no. 1 (February 2012): 12–14. https://doi.org/10.1016/j.jpag.2011.06.015.

Borjigen, Altangarvdi, Chi Huang, Mengxiang Lu, et al. "Status and Factors of Menstrual Knowledge, Attitudes, Behaviors and Their Correlation with Psychological Stress in Adolescent Girls." *Journal of Pediatric and Adolescent Gynecology* 32, no. 6 (December 2019): 584–89. https://doi.org/10.1016/j.jpag.2019.08.007.

Brensel, Lauren. "Pause the Period: State Bill Would Ban Mention of Menstruation in Elementary Schools." *Independent Florida Alligator*, March 27, 2023. https://www.alligator.org/article/2023/03/pause-the-period-state-bill-would-ban-mention-of-menstruation-in-elementary-schools.

Bülow, Anne, Andreas B. Neubauer, Bart Soenens, Savannah Boele, Jaap J. A. Denissen, and Loes Keijsers. "Universal Ingredients to Parenting Teens: Parental Warmth and Autonomy Support Promote Adolescent Well-Being in Most Families." *Scientific Reports* 12 (October 7, 2022): 16836. https://doi.org/10.1038/s41598-022-21071-0.

Centers for Disease Control and Prevention. "Epidemiological Notes and Reports Toxic-Shock Syndrome, United States, 1970–1982." *Morbidity and Mortality Weekly Report* 31, no. 16 (April 30, 1982): 201–4. https://www.cdc.gov/mmwr/preview/mmwrhtml/00000248.htm.

Chentsova Dutton, Yulia E., In-Jae Choi, and Eunsoo Choi. "Perceived Parental Support and Adolescents' Positive Self-Beliefs and Levels of Distress Across Four Countries." *Frontiers in Psychology* 11 (March 3, 2020): 353. https://doi.org/10.3389/fpsyg.2020.00353.

Common Sense Media. *Teens and Pornography: A New Research Report from Common Sense.* March 2022. https://www.commonsensemedia.org/sites/default/files/research/report/2022-teens-and-pornography-final-web.pdf.

Cottrell, Barbara Hansen. "Vaginal Douching." *Journal of Obstetric, Gynecologic & Neonatal Nursing* 32, no. 1 (January–February 2003): 12–18. https://doi.org/10.1177/0884217502239796.

Deardorff, Julianna, Heining Cham, Nancy A. Gonzales, et al. "Pubertal Timing and Mexican-Origin Girls' Internalizing and Externalizing Symptoms: The Influence of Harsh Parenting." *Developmental Psychology* 49, no. 9 (September 2013): 1790–804. https://doi.org/10.1037/a0031016.

DeGroff, Eric A. "Sex Education in the Public Schools and the Accommodation of Familial Rights." *Children's Legal Rights Journal* 26 (2006): 21. https://ssrn.com/abstract=1985251.

Diaz, Jaclyn. "Florida's Governor Signs Controversial Law Opponents Dubbed 'Don't Say Gay.'" NPR, March 28, 2022. https://www.npr.org/2022/03/28/1089221657/dont-say-gay-florida-desantis.

Digitale, Erin. "Age That Kids Acquire Mobile Phones Not Linked to Well-Being, Says

Stanford Medicine Study." Stanford Medicine News Center, November 21, 2022. https://med.stanford.edu/news/all-news/2022/11/children-mobile-phone-age.html.

Eisenberg, Marla, Jennifer Oliphant, Shari Plowman, Melanie Forstie, and Renee Sieving. "Increased Parent Support for Comprehensive Sexuality Education Over 15 Years." *Journal of Adolescent Health* 71, no. 6 (December 2022): 744–50. https://doi.org/10.1016/j.jadohealth.2022.08.005.

El-Hamamsy, Dina, Chanel Parmar, Stephanie Shoop-Worrall, and Fiona M. Reid. "Public Understanding of Female Genital Anatomy and Pelvic Organ Prolapse (POP): A Questionnaire-Based Pilot Study." *International Urogynecology Journal* 33, no. 2 (February 2022): 309–18. https://doi.org/10.1007/s00192-021-04727-9.

Emmanuel, Mickey, and Brooke R. Bokor. "Tanner Stages." In *StatPearls*. StatPearls Publishing, January 2025–. https://www.ncbi.nlm.nih.gov/books/NBK470280/.

Evans, Rebecca Lane, Bronwyn Harris, Chinwe Onuegbu, and Frances Griffiths. "Systematic Review of Educational Interventions to Improve the Menstrual Health of Young Adolescent Girls." *BMJ Open* 12, no. 6 (June 8, 2022): e057204. https://doi.org/10.1136/bmjopen-2021-057204.

Guan, Shu-Sha Angie, Julienne E. Bower, David M. Almeida, et al. "Parental Support Buffers the Association of Depressive Symptoms with Cortisol and C-Reactive Protein During Adolescence." *Brain, Behavior, and Immunity* 57 (October 2016): 134–43. https://doi.org/10.1016/j.bbi.2016.03.007.

Guttmacher Institute. "Evidence-Based Sex Education: The Case for Sustained Federal Support." Fact sheet, April 2025. https://www.guttmacher.org/fact-sheet/sex-education.

Guzikevits, Mika, Tom Gordon-Hecker, David Rekhtman, et al. "Sex Bias in Pain Management Decisions." *Proceedings of the National Academy of Sciences of the United States of America* 121, no. 33 (August 13, 2024): e2401331121. https://doi.org/10.1073/pnas.2401331121.

Hennegan, Julie, and Paul Montgomery. "Do Menstrual Hygiene Management Interventions Improve Education and Psychosocial Outcomes for Women and Girls in Low- and Middle-Income Countries? A Systematic Review." *PLOS One* 11, no. 2 (Feb 2016): e0146985. https://doi.org/10.1371/journal.pone.0146985.

Hewitt, Geri D., and Karen R. Gerancher. "Dysmenorrhea and Endometriosis in the Adolescent: ACOG Committee Opinion No. 760." *Obstetrics & Gynecology* 132, no. 6 (December 2018): e249–58. https://doi.org/10.1097/AOG.0000000000002978.

Hewitt, Geri D., and Jennie Yoost. "Gynecologic Management of Adolescents and Young Women with Seizure Disorders: ACOG Committee Opinion No. 806."

Obstetrics & Gynecology 135, no. 5 (May 2020): e213–20. https://doi.org/10.1097/AOG.0000000000003827.

Hopkins v. Hamden Board of Education. 29 Conn.Supp. 397, 289 A.2d 914 (1971). https://case-law.vlex.com/vid/hopkins-v-hamden-bd-890417521.

Hurst, Jeffrey L., Laura Widman, Julia Brasileiro, Anne J. Maheux, Reina Evans-Paulson, and Sophia Choukas-Bradley. "Parents' Attitudes Towards the Content of Sex Education in the USA: Associations with Religiosity and Political Orientation." *Sex Education* 24, no. 1 (January 2024): 108–24. https://doi.org/10.1080/14681811.2022.2162871.

Hwang, Juwon, and Catalina L. Toma. "The Role of Mental Well-Being and Perceived Parental Supportiveness in Adolescents' Problematic Internet Use: Moderation Analysis." *JMIR Mental Health* 8, no. 9 (September 2021): e26203. https://doi.org/10.2196/26203.

Jhe, Grace B., Laura J. Selby, Marissa C. Herzberg, Jenny Y. Ruan, Arianna L. D'Andrea, Olivia N. Katalinic, Victoria A. Harper, and Maria C. Terras. "Pornography Use Among Adolescents and the Role of Primary Care." *Family Medicine and Community Health* 11, no. 1 (January 2023): e001776. https://doi.org/10.1136/fmch-2022-001776

Ju, Hong, Mark Jones, and Gita Mishra. "The Prevalence and Risk Factors of Dysmenorrhea." *Epidemiologic Reviews* 36, no. 1 (2014): 104–13. https://doi.org/10.1093/epirev/mxt009.

Kardaş, Burcu, Ömer Kardaş, Meliha Demiral, and Mehmet Nuri Özbek. "Early Puberty Paradox: An Investigation of Anxiety Levels of Mothers and Children, Children's Quality of Life, and Psychiatric Diagnoses." *European Journal of Pediatrics* 182, no. 8 (August 2023): 3775–83. https://doi.org/10.1007/s00431-023-05057-2.

Keizer, Renske, Katrien O. W. Helmerhorst, and Loes van Rijn-van Gelderen. "Perceived Quality of the Mother-Adolescent and Father-Adolescent Attachment Relationship and Adolescents' Self-Esteem." *Journal of Youth and Adolescence* 48, no. 6 (2019): 1203–17. https://doi.org/10.1007/s10964-019-01007-0.

Lacroix, Amy E., Hurria Gondal, Karlie R. Shumway, and Michelle D. Langaker. "Physiology, Menarche." In *StatPearls*. StatPearls Publishing, January 2025–. https://www.ncbi.nlm.nih.gov/books/NBK470216/.

Lindberg, Laura D., Melissa K. Kearney, Isaac Maddow-Zimet, and Nicole K. Smith. "Adolescents' Receipt of Sex Education in a Nationally Representative Sample, 2011–2019." *Journal of Adolescent Health* 70, no. 2 (February 2022): 290–97. https://doi.org/10.1016/j.jadohealth.2021.08.027.

Maharaj, Trisha, and Inga T. Winkler. "Transnational Engagements: Cultural and Religious Practices Related to Menstruation." In *The Palgrave Handbook of Critical Menstruation Studies*, edited by Chris Bobel, Inga T. Winkler, Breanne Fahs, Katie Ann Hasson, Elizabeth Arveda Kissling, and Tomi-Ann Roberts. Palgrave Macmillan, 2020. https://www.ncbi.nlm.nih.gov/books/NBK565655/.

Marroquin, Joanna, Marianthi-Anna Kiomourtzoglou, Alexandra Scranton, and Anna Z. Pollack. "Chemicals in Menstrual Products: A Systematic Review." *BJOG: An International Journal of Obstetrics and Gynaecology* 131, no. 5 (April 2024): 655–64. https://doi.org/10.1111/1471–0528.17668.

Medina-Perucha, Laura, Tomàs López-Jiménez, Anna Sofie Holst, et al. "Use and Perceptions on Reusable and Non-Reusable Menstrual Products in Spain: A Mixed-Methods Study." *PLOS One* 17, no. 3 (March 17, 2022): e0265646. https://doi.org/10.1371/journal.pone.0265646.

Mills-Koonce, W. Roger, Peter D. Rehder, and Amy L. McCurdy. "The Significance of Parenting and Parent-Child Relationships for Sexual and Gender Minority Adolescents." *Journal of Research on Adolescence* 28, no. 3 (September 2018): 637–49. https://doi.org/10.1111/jora.12404.

Mishori, Ranit, Hope Ferdowsian, Keren Naimer, Morgan Volpellier, and Thomas McHale. "The Little Tissue That Couldn't: Dispelling Myths About the Hymen's Role in Determining Sexual History and Assault." *Reproductive Health* 16, no. 1 (June 3, 2019): 74. https://doi.org/10.1186/s12978-019-0731-8.

Morales, Alexandra, Mireia Orgilés, and José P. Espada. "Sexually Unexperienced Adolescents Benefit the Most from a Sexual Education Program for Adolescents: A Longitudinal Cluster Randomized Controlled Study." *AIDS Education and Prevention* 32, no. 6 (December 2020): 493–511. https://doi.org/10.1521/aeap.2020.32.6.493.

Noonan, Jacqueline A. "A History of Pediatric Specialties: The Development of Pediatric Cardiology." *Pediatric Research* 56, no. 2 (August 2004): 298–306. https://doi.org/10.1203/01.PDR.0000132662.73362.96.

Parris, Mehruba Anwar, Maryann Mazer-Amirshahi, Diane P. Calello, and Andrew Stolbach. "ACMT Position Statement: No Evidence That Tampons Cause Metal Poisoning." American College of Medical Toxicology. October 2, 2024. https://www.acmt.net/news/acmt-position-statement-no-evidence-that-tampons-cause-metal-poisoning/.

Patnam, Radhika, Autumn Edenfield, and Steven Swift. "Defining Normal Apical Vaginal Support: A Relook at the POSST Study." *International Urogynecology Journal* 30 (2019): 45–51. https://doi.org/10.1007/s00192-018-3681-8.

Period.org. "State of the Period 2023." 2023. https://period.org/uploads/2023-State-of-the-Period-Study.pdf.

Planned Parenthood. "History of Sex Education in the U.S." February 9, 2017. https://www.plannedparenthood.org/uploads/filer_public/da/67/da67fd5d-631d-438a-85e8-a446d90fd1e3/20170209_sexed_d04_1.pdf.

Rafferty, Jason. "Gender Identity Development in Children." HealthyChildren.org. Last updated May 7, 2024. https://www.healthychildren.org/English/ages-stages/gradeschool/Pages/Gender-Identity-and-Gender-Confusion-In-Children.aspx.

Rasing, Sanne P. A., Daan H. M. Creemers, Jan M. A. M. Janssens, and Ron H. J. Scholte. "The Association Between Perceived Maternal and Paternal Psychopathology and Depression and Anxiety Symptoms in Adolescent Girls." *Frontiers in Psychology* 6 (July 21, 2015): 963. https://doi.org/10.3389/fpsyg.2015.00963.

Ratliff, Emma L., Amanda S. Morris, Lixian Cui, Jens E. Jespersen, Jennifer S. Silk, and Michael M. Criss. "Supportive Parent-Adolescent Relationships as a Foundation for Adolescent Emotion Regulation and Adjustment." *Frontiers in Psychology* 14 (2023): 1193449. https://doi.org/10.3389/fpsyg.2023.1193449.

Reynolds, Rachel V., Howa Yeung, Carol E. Cheng, et al. "Guidelines of Care for the Management of Acne Vulgaris." *Journal of the American Academy of Dermatology* 90, no. 5 (2024): 1006.e1–1006.e30. https://doi.org/10.1016/j.jaad.2023.12.017.

Sadoughi, Majid. "Overparenting and Adolescent's Trait Anxiety: Unraveling the Roles of Basic Psychological Needs Frustration and Emotion Dysregulation." *Acta Psychologica* 251 (November 2024): 104579. https://doi.org/10.1016/j.actpsy.2024.104579.

Sahin, Nilfer, Burcu Kasap, Ulviye Kirli, Nese Yeniceri, and Yasar Topal. "Assessment of Anxiety-Depression Levels and Perceptions of Quality of Life in Adolescents with Dysmenorrhea." *Reproductive Health* 15, no. 1 (January 26, 2018): 13. https://doi.org/10.1186/s12978-018-0453-3.

Schmitt, Margaret L., Caitlin Gruer, Christine Hagstrom, et al. "'It Always Gets Pushed Aside:' Qualitative Perspectives on Puberty and Menstruation Education in U.S.A. Schools." *Frontiers in Reproductive Health* 4 (October 21, 2022): 1018217. https://doi.org/10.3389/frph.2022.1018217.

Shaaban, Omar M., Alaa Eldin A. Youssef, Mostafa M. Khodry, and Sayed A. Mostafa. "Vaginal Douching by Women with Vulvovaginitis and Relation to Reproductive Health Hazards." *BMC Women's Health* 13 (May 14, 2013): 23. https://doi.org/10.1186/1472-6874-13-23.

Shah, Vishna, Wolf Schmidt, Bakary Sonko, Julie Hennegan, Penelope Phillips-Howard, and Belen Torondel. "Effect of a Multicomponent Intervention to Improve Menstrual Health and Hygiene and School Attendance Among Adolescent Girls in the Gambia (MEGAMBO Trial)." *Journal of Adolescent Health* 76, no. 5 (May 2025): 879–88. https://doi.org/10.1016/j.jadohealth.2024.12.018.

Shearston, Jenni A., Kristen Upson, Milo Gordon, et al. "Tampons as a Source of Exposure to Metal(loid)s." *Environment International* 190 (August 2024): 108849. https://doi.org/10.1016/j.envint.2024.108849.

Shenkman, Julia L., Leah C. Neubauer, Linda Mason, et al. "Building Menstrual Health and Hygiene-Supportive Environments: Exploring Teachers' Experience in Rural Western Kenya." *Frontiers in Public Health* 11 (July 25, 2023): 1206069. https://doi.org/10.3389/fpubh.2023.1206069.

Shibeshi, Bikis Yaynie, Amanu Aragaw Emiru, and Melash Belacehew Asresie. "Disparities in Menstrual Hygiene Management Between Urban and Rural Schoolgirls in Northeast, Ethiopia." *PLOS One* 16, no. 9 (September 30, 2021): e0257853. https://doi.org/10.1371/journal.pone.0257853.

Singh, Devendra Raj, Shreesha Shrestha, Kshitij Karki, et al. "Parental Knowledge and Communication with Their Adolescent on Sexual and Reproductive Health Issues in Nepal." *PLOS One* 18, no.7 (July 2023): e0289116. https://doi.org/10.1371/journal.pone.0289116.

Skeith, Leslie, and Shannon M. Bates. "Estrogen, Progestin, and Beyond: Thrombotic Risk and Contraceptive Choices." *Hematology: American Society of Hematology Education Program* 2024, no. 1 (December 6, 2024): 644–51. https://doi.org/10.1182/hematology.2024000591.

Smith, T. W., and J. Son. *General Social Survey 2012 Final Report: Trends in Public Attitudes About Sexual Morality*. NORC at the University of Chicago, 2013. https://www.norc.org/content/dam/norc-org/pdfs/Trends%20in%20Sexual%20Moraility_Final.pdf.

Sørensen, S., N. Brix, A. Ernst, L. L. B. Lauridsen, and C. H. Ramlau-Hansen. "Maternal Age at Menarche and Pubertal Development in Sons and Daughters: A Nationwide Cohort Study." *Human Reproduction* 33, no. 11 (November 2018): 2043–50. https://doi.org/10.1093/humrep/dey287.

Szucs, Leigh E., Christopher R. Harper, Jack Andrzejewski, Lisa C. Barrios, Leah Robin, and Pete Hunt. "Overwhelming Support for Sexual Health Education in U.S. Schools: A Meta-Analysis of 23 Surveys Conducted Between 2000 and 2016." *Journal of Adolescent Health* 70, no. 4 (April 2022): 598–606. https://doi.org/10.1016/j.jadohealth.2021.05.016.

Tang, Jingyi, Peng Xue, Xiaoxia Huang, Cuilan Lin, and Shijian Liu. "Diet and Nutrients Intakes During Infancy and Childhood in Relation to Early Puberty: A Systematic Review and Meta-Analysis." *Nutrients* 14, no. 23 (2022): 5004. https://doi.org/10.3390/nu14235004.

Vostral, Sharra L. "Rely and Toxic Shock Syndrome: A Technological Health Crisis." *Yale Journal of Biology and Medicine* 84, no. 4 (December 2011): 447–59. https://www.ncbi.nlm.nih.gov/pmc/articles/PMC3238331/.

Weissfeld, Alice S. "The History of Tampons: From Ancient Times to an FDA-Regulated Medical Device." *Clinical Microbiology Newsletter* 32, no. 10 (May 2010): 73–76. https://doi.org/10.1016/j.clinmicnews.2010.04.003.

White, Rebecca M. B., Julianna Deardorff, and Nancy A. Gonzales. "Contextual Amplification or Attenuation of Pubertal Timing Effects on Depressive Symptoms Among Mexican American Girls." *Journal of Adolescent Health* 50, no. 6 (June 2012): 565–71. https://doi.org/10.1016/j.jadohealth.2011.10.006.

Wolff, Mary S., Julie A. Britton, Lisa Boguski, et al. "Environmental Exposures and

Puberty in Inner-City Girls." *Environmental Research* 107, no. 3 (July 2008): 393–400. https://doi.org/10.1016/j.envres.2008.03.006.

World Health Organization. "Comprehensive Sexuality Education." May 18, 2023. https://www.who.int/news-room/questions-and-answers/item/comprehensive-sexuality-education.

Yang, Bo, Truls Ostbye, Xin Huang, et al. "Maternal Age at Menarche and Pubertal Timing in Boys and Girls: A Cohort Study from Chongqing, China." *Journal of Adolescent Health* 68, no. 3 (March 2021): 508–16. https://doi.org/10.1016/j.jadohealth.2020.06.036.

Yap, Marie B. H., Pamela D. Pilkington, Siobhan M. Ryan, Claire M. Kelly, and Anthony F. Jorm. "Parenting Strategies for Reducing the Risk of Adolescent Depression and Anxiety Disorders: A Delphi Consensus Study." *Journal of Affective Disorders* 156 (March 2014): 67–75. https://doi.org/10.1016/j.jad.2013.11.017.

Zhang, Lanlan, Elizabeth A. Reynolds Losin, Yoni K. Ashar, Leonie Koban, and Tor D. Wager. "Gender Biases in Estimation of Others' Pain." *Journal of Pain* 22, no. 9 (September 2021): 1048–59. https://doi.org/10.1016/j.jpain.2021.03.001.

Zhang, Qi, and Wongeun Ji. "Overparenting and Offspring Depression, Anxiety, and Internalizing Symptoms: A Meta-Analysis." *Development and Psychopathology* 36, no. 3 (2024): 1307–22. https://doi.org/10.1017/s095457942300055x.

Index

T

U

V

W

Y

Acknowledgments

As a child, I didn't consider myself much of a writer. While my papers and short stories always received good grades, I never enjoyed the process. It felt almost painful to have to turn my complex emotions and abstract thoughts into organized paragraphs that met grammatical and style standards. So, when I did write, I did so because I had to. But writing changed for me when I enrolled in AP English at Smiths Station High School. It was in this class that I truly learned the art of writing. Mrs. Jean Lowther taught me how to use writing as a tool for emotional expression, detailed explanation, and unlimited imagination. Because of her expert instruction, my weakness became a strength, and my writing made way for public speaking, content creation, and this book. Thank you, Mrs. Lowther.

Writing *The Period & Puberty Parenting Revolution* has been one of the most challenging and rewarding endeavors of my life. Shortly after completing my medical training, I felt the urge to write a book. I didn't know how or when it would happen, but I knew I needed to share the knowledge and expertise I had gained with people well beyond the walls of the hospital and clinic. In the meantime, I focused on building a social media presence as The Period Doctor, where I could educate and advocate for people with periods, especially adolescents and children. The platform grew rapidly, with my content reaching millions of people and positively affecting those of all ages. That's when Morgan Strehlow reached out to me. She saw the potential for authorship within me when it was still just a quiet hope and whispered prayer. With her incredible guidance, we went from just an idea to the book you hold in your hands today. Thank you, Morgan.

I also wouldn't have written this book without the love and support of my family. To my father, thank you for always believing in me, even when you didn't fully understand the vision. Thank you for not judging me when I decided to train in a lesser-known subspecialty, or when I "retired" from obstetrics, or when I left a perfectly good hospital-employed position to try my hand at full-time entrepreneurship. Thank you for stepping in as my main supporter and encourager after Mama passed. From documentary screenings to keynote addresses, panels, and award ceremonies, you have made sure that your daughter had a physical parent present to cheer her on. Thank you.

To my brother, thank you for listening to and reading chapter drafts. Thank you for always seeing qualities in me that I sometimes doubted. Thank you for encouraging me to use my voice to challenge the status quo and be a relentless champion for justice. To my sisters, thank you for being my listening ears, my voices of reason, and my biggest cheerleaders. From the very beginning, I confided my fears, my hopes, and my struggles in you, and you were never too busy or too tired when I called on you for help. Before I was a doctor, let alone The Period Doctor, you knew me fully. Thank you for reminding me of who I am and whose I am. Thank you for hyping me up when I needed to step it up and lovingly correcting me when I needed to chill out. You are my secret weapons, and your presence in my life is what makes me feel the most unstoppable.

Thank you to Spelman College for the freedom, sisterhood, confidence, and presence that you have given me. For four years, I was free to learn, live, and exist within your safety, protection, and care. There's no other place in the world where I would have developed so fully into the person I am today. It was there that I learned that I was a thought leader and realized leadership didn't have to be loud, overbearing, or selfish. I learned it could be quiet, it could be gentle, and it could serve. From the late Dr. Jane E. Smith, I learned the invaluable and immeasurable power of transparency. I learned that the most successful women who I desperately admired had imperfect lives that made them no less impressive and no less worthy. And it was at Spelman that I met my lifelong friends—my friends who pray for me, check on me, hold me accountable, and hold me close. Thank you, Spelman.

Thank you to my husband, who decided to do life with me while fully understanding that I am as anxious as I am ambitious. He understood that I would never be satisfied with a life where I didn't serve, advocate, and educate others. He understood that I desired a soft life but would be taking the hard path to get there. He has loved me as the girl I have always been, the woman I'm becoming, the wife I try to be, and the mother I am. Thank you, Zachary, for never saying a dream or goal is "too big." Thank you for being my biggest supporter, my partner, and my friend. My joy is your joy, and my accomplishments are ours to share. Thank you for letting me be me and never asking me to quiet my voice or dim my light.

Thank you to my sweet baby boy, Joshua. From the womb, you have developed and grown right alongside this book. I wrote most of these pages while pregnant and immediately postpartum with you. On the days when things felt too heavy to bear, your kicks and then your gentle coos were what kept me going. Your laughs are the sweetest sounds I've ever heard, and the sight of your smile is more special than that of a shooting star. It is my deepest hope that one day you will know that your mother doesn't shy away from hard things—that she pursues her wildest dreams and goes after her greatest goals. I hope one day you are half as proud of me as I am of you. My greatest joy, by far, is being your mom.

And finally, thank you to my readers. You somehow found this book and decided to take a chance on a first-time author who had the audacity to call for a parenting revolution. I value every single one of you and hope that these pages have inspired you to show up fully as the irreplaceable reproductive health advocates that you are.

About the Author

Danyel Jones of Marquiś Productions

Dr. Charis Chambers is a physician, speaker, and reproductive health advocate. After becoming a board certified ob-gyn, she completed fellowship training and obtained specialty certification in pediatric and adolescent gynecology. She is the creator of The Period Doctor, where she explains taboo topics, offers expert opinions, and provides education on menstruation and gynecological health. Dr. Chambers received her bachelor's degree from Spelman College and her medical degree from the University of Alabama's School of Medicine. Dr. Chambers lives in Atlanta, Georgia, with her husband and son.